LENTEN AWAKENING
DAILY MEDITATIONS FROM ASH WEDNESDAY TO EASTER

Phil Needham

CREST BOOKS

Copyright © 2020 by The Salvation Army

Published by Crest Books

Crest Books
The Salvation Army National Headquarters
615 Slaters Lane
Alexandria, VA 22313
Phone: 703/684-5523

Lt. Col. Tim Foley, *National Program Secretary and Editor-in-Chief*
Alexanderia Saurman, *Editorial Assistant*
Ashley C. Schena, *Graphic Designer*

ISBN: 978-1-946709-16-5

All rights reserved. No part of this publication may be reproduced, stored in a retrieval system, or transmitted in any form or by any means without prior written permission of the publisher. Exceptions are brief quotations in printed reviews.

Contents

The Season of Lent 1
How to Take This Journey 5

ASH WEDNESDAY
The Courage to Remember and Repent 7

THURSDAY AFTER ASH WEDNESDAY
Finding Our Memories 11

FRIDAY AFTER ASH WEDNESDAY
Faith Shaped by Memories 15

SATURDAY AFTER ASH WEDNESDAY
Memories of Jesus 19

SUNDAY THE FIRST WEEK OF LENT
Jesus Revealing Us 23

MONDAY THE FIRST WEEK OF LENT
Revealing Our Sin 27

TUESDAY THE FIRST WEEK OF LENT
Revealing Our Forgiveness 31

WEDNESDAY THE FIRST WEEK OF LENT
Revealing Our Homelessness 35

THURSDAY THE FIRST WEEK OF LENT
Revealing Our Community 39

FRIDAY THE FIRST WEEK OF LENT
Revealing Our Mission 43

SATURDAY THE FIRST WEEK OF LENT
Revealing Our Future 47

SUNDAY THE SECOND WEEK OF LENT
Jesus Humbling Us 51

MONDAY THE SECOND WEEK OF LENT
Seeing the Nothings 57

TUESDAY THE SECOND WEEK OF LENT
Claiming the Real Somethings 61

WEDNESDAY THE SECOND WEEK OF LENT
Beginning Again 65

THURSDAY THE SECOND WEEK OF LENT
Trusting 69

FRIDAY THE SECOND WEEK OF LENT
Risking Transparency... 73

SATURDAY THE SECOND WEEK OF LENT
Living Without Excess 77

SUNDAY THE THIRD WEEK OF LENT
Jesus Healing Us..81

MONDAY THE THIRD WEEK OF LENT
Soul Healing.. 85

TUESDAY THE THIRD WEEK OF LENT
Emotional Healing 89

WEDNESDAY THE THIRD WEEK OF LENT
Relational Healing 93

THURSDAY THE THIRD WEEK OF LENT
Physical Healing 97

FRIDAY THE THIRD WEEK OF LENT
Church Healing 101

SATURDAY THE THIRD WEEK OF LENT
Inclusive Healing 105

SUNDAY THE FOURTH WEEK OF LENT
Jesus Re-Creating Us 109

MONDAY THE FOURTH WEEK OF LENT
Jesus Re-Creating Our Heart 115

TUESDAY THE FOURTH WEEK OF LENT
Recreating Our Body 119

WEDNESDAY THE FOURTH WEEK OF LENT
Re-Creating Our Spiritual Practice 123

THURSDAY THE FOURTH WEEK OF LENT
Re-Creating Our Purpose 127

FRIDAY THE FOURTH WEEK OF LENT
Re-Creating Our Spiritual Family 131

SATURDAY THE FOURTH WEEK OF LENT
Re-Creating Our World 135

SUNDAY THE FIFTH WEEK OF LENT
Jesus Uniting Us 139

MONDAY THE FIFTH WEEK OF LENT
Suffering Together 145

TUESDAY THE FIFTH WEEK OF LENT
Singing Together 149

WEDNESDAY THE FIFTH WEEK OF LENT
Drawing Closer Together 153

THURSDAY THE FIFTH WEEK OF LENT
Maturing Together 157

FRIDAY THE FIFTH WEEK OF LENT
Sharing Everything Together 161

SATURDAY THE FIFTH WEEK OF LENT
Conspiring Together 165

HOLY WEEK
Walking the Last Week with Jesus 169

PALM SUNDAY THE SIXTH WEEK OF LENT
Riding a Donkey 171

MONDAY OF HOLY WEEK
Clearing Temples 175

TUESDAY OF HOLY WEEK
Washing Feet 179

WEDNESDAY OF HOLY WEEK
Breaking His Heart.. 183

THURSDAY OF HOLY WEEK
Being Thirsty 189

GOOD FRIDAY
Gifting Paradise 195

HOLY SATURDAY
Tasting Death 199

EASTER SUNDAY
Resurrection Awakening 205

The Season of Lent

The word "lent" comes from an old English word meaning "spring." In the Christian calendar, it refers to the forty days before Easter (excluding Sundays). Because the number of days in Lent is fixed, the Lenten Season always commences on the Wednesday before the first of the five Sundays before Easter Sunday. Rarely, then, does that Wednesday have the same calendar date.

Lent has traditionally—and helpfully—been observed as a time of spiritual meditation, self-discipline, penitence, prayer, and fasting. Today, some branches of the Christian church observe it with prescribed rituals and clearly defined spiritual disciplines. Other churches observe the season with less formality. In these meditations, we won't discuss issues of external observance. Rather, we shall take the opportunity to focus on Jesus. If there is anything all who claim to be Christians can agree on, it is that calling Jesus our Lord and Rabbi means that his life and his teaching are our guides for living. In other words, we look at and assess our own lives through the lens of how he actually lived and what he actually taught. Does it even need saying that such comparisons, when made honestly, reveal that we fall short?

What then do we do? Do we become spiritual defeatists who continually ask for forgiveness while dismissing God's ability to bring about needed change in our lives? No, we trust the Spirit's sanctifying power to make us more like Jesus. The Season of Lent is an opportunity to do exactly that over a period of forty-six days (including Sundays), leading right up to Easter.

Lent, in fact, has Easter in mind. It invites us to a journey of self-assessment and repentance that prepares us to receive the risen Christ and empowers us to live our lives as victorious Easter people. There is work to be done in all our lives. So, welcome to Lent! Welcome to the opportunity to spend time with Jesus, where your sin can meet his righteousness, your failures his forgiveness, your weakness his strength.

Our Lenten journey together will focus on Jesus. We will recall events from his life and ministry: his self-giving love, the singular thrust of his life toward obedience to God's will and purpose, the pain he endured for us, the radical teaching he expects his followers to live by. With greater depth and consequence, we will claim him as our Savior. We will turn the pages of the Gospels to rediscover this man from Nazareth. We will ask the age-old question: Who is he? We will find ourselves captivated by the age-old answer: "Tis the Lord, the King of Glory!" And we will respond: "At his feet we humbly fall, Crown him, crown him Lord of all!"

The title of the book was given to me by my wife, Keitha, who has been both my proofreader and my consultant. After having read the full manuscript, she suggested the title *Lenten Awakening*. She felt that what the meditations were seeking to do was to expose the life and teaching of Jesus in such a way as to awaken us out of our complacencies and encourage us to see ourselves through his eyes.

As we take this journey together, we will see Jesus calling us to repentance, and we will own our need to confess our sin. We will allow ourselves to come under his revealing gaze and become more aware of what we could not see in ourselves and what we can still become. We will sit at the feet of this humble teacher and repent of our disabling arrogance. We will marvel at the many dimensions of Jesus' healing ministry, thank him for our own healings—some of them ongoing—and perhaps pray for a needed new healing. As we explore Jesus' ongoing mission of re-creation in our lives and in the world, we will hear him invite us to be a part of it. We will see how God's mission to "bring all things together in Christ" (Ephesians 1:10) calls us, his disciples, to the ministry of reconciliation. And as we walk with Jesus through the last week of his earthly life, through crucifixion to resurrection, we will claim again the saving and sanctifying power of Calvary love and Easter life.

I pray these reflections will draw you to Jesus, as I have been drawn. I hope they will awaken you to what he sees in you and in the world. And I hope they will help you find the Way on your journey as his disciple.

How to Take This Journey

This book of meditations is an invitation to prayer-walk with Jesus. As you embark on this journey, you will see Jesus at work, awakening people to see what he sees, hear what he says, and do what he does. He will invite you, the reader, to participate in the awakening.

Jesus' teachings are important to anyone who decides to be his disciple. He did not, however, come to fill our brains with information. He came to pierce our hearts with his passion and arouse our being with the character of his life. He came to see what is in us, and with his seeing, help us to see ourselves as we really are. He came to affirm us as we've never been affirmed before, and at the same time, show us our incredible capacity to grow closer in likeness to him. In other words, he frees us to confess our sin because such honesty is the first step forward from where we are.

There are basically three parts to each meditation. The first is suggested Scripture passages for reflection in preparation for the meditation. They relate to the subject of the meditation, though they may not be specifically referenced in the meditation. I suggest you read these passages first, maybe even offer a prayer the words may call you to. The second part is the meditation itself, which is designed to stimulate and challenge your own reflection around the subject of the meditation. The third part is a concluding prayer, shaped by the Scripture and the meditation, which you are invited to pray for yourself. You may want to add to the prayer or pray in your own words.

It is important that this time of meditation takes place in a controlled setting where interruptions are less likely to distract you. For many, that time would be in the early morning. For others for whom private space is next to impossible at that time of day, other arrangements can be made.

Although the meditations are designed for your private devotions, it may be desirable for a very small group—for example, a married couple, a group of friends—to do the devotions together, followed by a time of sharing. Two to four people could actually do them together through a scheduled conference call or Zoom meeting each day. Perhaps a group of people who are doing the meditations alone could meet or do the conference call or Zoom meeting once a week and share what the week's journey has meant to them and to pray together for each other. Please use these meditations as you need to!

ASH WEDNESDAY
The Courage to Remember and Repent

Scripture for Reflection: Hebrews 12:1-2

What do you remember? The answer to that question would say a lot about what has shaped your life. Of course, most of our memories are repressed and unavailable to our consciousness. I'm a long way from figuring out why we remember some things and not others. I am mystified by my own difficulty in recalling the details of many important events in my life, while I can remember to perfection some of the most trivial things you can imagine—or maybe they aren't so trivial.

Just because some of our memories are repressed, we cannot claim they've been removed. All of them are stored in our brains, and unless there has been actual physical damage to the brain, they still reside there somewhere among those millions of brain cells. So, what causes us to remember some things from our past and not others? There are certainly no easy answers to that question. It does seem, however, that some people remember mostly the good stuff and feel more positive about their lives, and others remember mostly the bad stuff and feel they haven't been given the breaks that others have. Memories can be a source of assuring reinforcement or menacing defeatism—good memories or painful ones.

There are three things we can do with our painful memories. We can repress them as if they never happened. We can turn them loose on ourselves and allow them to undermine our sense of self-worth and our personal confidence. Or we can learn from them and turn that knowledge into strength.

What if the painful memories relate to sins we have committed against others? We confess them before the person we wronged, and we seek the grace of her forgiveness. If we sin against ourselves, we seek the grace to forgive ourselves. The important thing to keep in our minds and treasure in our hearts is that we are not alone in any of this. It all happens in the presence of God, because as the psalmist David knew, all sins are sin against God (Psalm 51:4); they are violations of who he intended us to be. We repent before him. He forgives us, whether or not the person we sinned against does, and whether or not we forgive ourselves.

As we reflect on the story of Jesus this Lenten Season, we must not only bring with us a willingness to seek forgiveness from the one we may have wronged, but we must also confess those sins to God, fall to our knees before him, and ask for his forgiveness. Many branches of the Christian church observe the commencement of Lent by making the sign of the cross with ashes on the forehead of worshippers. In the Bible, ashes symbolize repentance (Job 42:6). When used to form a cross, they become a call to remember Jesus' crucifixion. By bearing the ashen sign of the cross on their foreheads, worshippers are saying that they themselves bear the blame.

Centuries ago, some churches used to sing a hymn during Lent that opened with the question: "O thou wretched Judas, what hast thou now done?" Was Judas the only one to blame? Fortunately, the hymn is rarely sung, if at all. It excludes all the other guilty people; it excludes you and me. More to the point was another hymn. Here are some of the words: "Who was the guilty? Who brought this upon Thee? Alas, my treason, Jesus, hath undone Thee…'Twas I, Lord Jesus, I it was denied Thee: *I crucified Thee*" (italics added). "He was wounded for *our* transgressions" (Isaiah 53:5, italics added).

The true saints of God never forget their guilt. They never forget they are saved by grace. As John Wesley lay dying, he summed up his own claims with these words:

> What have I to trust to for salvation? I can see nothing that I have done or suffered that will bear looking at. I have no other plea than this: I the chief of sinner am, but Jesus died for me.

This Jesus poured out his life for us in a cruel crucifixion too ugly for us to imagine. But in that tortuous death was released in full force the saving compassion of God. We must ask, "for what reason?" For good reason: to open the door to our becoming who God meant for us to be. Jesus was crucified so that he could live in us and enable us to begin looking like him. Behold, Jesus our model for living. Do we have the courage to look at him, to see the great distance we have yet to travel to have any resemblance to him?

Lent calls us to have the courage to claim the ashes of our repentance, receive God's forgiveness through the crucified Jesus, and move our lives closer to Christlikeness.

Prayer
Dear Lord, I confess I am unworthy of your love, undeserving of your forgiveness, and incapable of being a credible disciple of Jesus on my own. By the merits of Jesus' death, I repent of my sinful failures (here the reader may want to specify one or some of those failures), and I receive by faith the gift of my next step forward toward Christlikeness. In the name of Jesus, please Lord, help me to take that next step. Amen.

THURSDAY AFTER ASH WEDNESDAY
Finding Our Memories

Scripture for Reflection: Deuteronomy 32:7-11

In one way or another, our memories shape our lives. How this happens depends on how we relate to them. If we think we can simply cast them aside and start all over with a totally clean slate, we are fooling ourselves. Our memories shape us in ways both good and bad. It depends on what we do with them.

If we cling to memories of being run over, manipulated, and taken advantage of, those memories will control us. We will read them into just about everything. New situations will in one way or another be seen as a replay of the same tapes. We will accept the role of the abused and be a victim. Or we will be ever suspicious of people's motives and shape our responses accordingly, to the detriment of building trusting relationships. Neither is helpful to our spiritual growth.

On the other hand, we can see our past through rose-colored lens. This kind of remembering soothes our dissatisfaction with the present by contrasting it with an idealized past, the so called "good old days." This glorified past serves to hide our failure to deal with the present; it shifts the blame from ourselves. There is always some lack of truth in this way of remembering. The past never was as glorious as we so often portray it. The petition of a hymn writer is well worth adopting: "Lord, cleanse my memory, mind and will." Our idolatry of the past immobilizes us in the present and robs us of the future. Since we find we cannot now have the past exactly as it was, we give up and live in nostalgia and regret. We become paralyzed. And our paralysis in the present leaves us ill-prepared for the future.

By the time you read this, I will have reached the age of eighty. I have more past in my earthly life than I have future—and the present seems to be moving at an incredibly fast rate. Sometimes I feel outdated and occasionally even useless. For example, I'd rather read a book in my hands rather than on a screen, though I celebrate the exponential increase in the availability of books through the internet. I'd rather preach (or hear) a sermon that is person-to-person rather than person-to-screen-to-person, though I am fully aware we live in an increasingly visual culture and must honor that reality.

It is not my calling to reject e-books or sermons with visuals. But I can remember a time when books had a lasting impact, and we would go back to them again and again because they were foundational for our lives. I am concerned about a world where the book fad of the day comes and goes so quickly in Christian circles. I am also concerned about the highly manipulative possibilities of visual technology and the demand that church services always be entertaining. If we seek to live exclusively in the ever-changing "Now," we lose our memory. "If we forget the past," someone has said, "we are doomed to repeat it."

The Bible invites us to claim our memories. It is a book of memories, and its readers are challenged not to forget them. Your life is a book of memories. Learn from them, the good and the bad, the painful ones and the fulfilling ones—and let God teach you, heal you, and sanctify you as you claim them. Remember the ways the Lord delivered you in times of trouble (Psalm 77:11-20). Remember the compassionate commands of our Lord (Acts 20:35). Remember Jesus, and pray for the grace and strength to live out the life to which he has called you (Luke 24:44-48).

Prayer

Dear Lord, I thank you for the ability to remember how you have been present with me over my years, even when I didn't know it or understand it at the time. I thank you for the ways my memories help me understand myself. I thank you for the positive memories that have enriched my life and for the painful memories that have taught me, driven me to my knees, and now strengthen me. Above all, I thank you for the memories of Jesus, the memories that define and grace my life. Help me to keep those memories before me as I live this day for your honor and glory. Amen.

FRIDAY AFTER ASH WEDNESDAY
Faith Shaped by Memories

Scripture for Reflection: Psalm 105:1-6; Ephesians 2:1-13

The Bible is a book of sacred memories. Like our own memories, it is selective in its recall—it doesn't try to remember everything. It remembers what God wants remembered. The people of Israel, for example, were told specifically what to remember:

> My father was a starving Aramean. He went down to Egypt, living as an immigrant there with few family members, but that is where he became a great nation, mighty and numerous. The Egyptians treated us terribly, oppressing us and forcing hard labor on us. So we cried out for help to the Lord…The Lord heard our call. God saw our misery, our trouble, and our oppression. The Lord brought us out of Egypt with a strong hand and an outstretched arm…He brought us to this place and gave us this land—a land full of milk and honey. (Deuteronomy 26:5b-9)

Every year they were to remember this miraculous deliverance by offering the Passover sacrifice and eating unleavened bread for six days (Deuteronomy 16:1-8). The psalmist invites these offspring of Abraham and Jacob to remember the marvelous works done by the Lord (Psalm 105:5-6). The Old Testament ends with the command to remember the instructions from Moses (Malachi 4:4).

The Jewish faith is grounded in memory, to this very day. So is the Christian faith. Jesus, a devout Jew and a rabbi, understood the significance of what he said and did, and he trusted his disciples to remember. He knew they would remember a miracle at a wedding in Cana, a feeding of five thousand, a sermon on a mount, a startling healing of a demoniac. None of his disciples were with him during his desert temptations, but he told them about it so they'd have it to remember. He knew they would remember a face set steadfastly to go to Jerusalem for a redemptive death. He knew they would remember a gathering storm, an intimate last supper together, an arrest, their own cowardice, a cross, a resurrection, a commissioning.

The New Testament church was also called to remember Jesus. In his farewell sermon to the Ephesian elders, the apostle Paul tells them to "remember the words of the Lord Jesus" (Acts 20:35). Paul tells the Philippian church to remember Christ's self-humbling and self-emptying love and to model their own relationships accordingly (Philippians 2:1-11). And Gentile Christians are admonished to remember that when they were excluded from the Covenant, the crucified Christ opened the closed borders, now bringing them, the formerly excluded, into the one church family.

Our most precious memories are of people important to us. We recount things about them, experiences we shared with them, as treasures. The memories are precious because the persons are precious, and the memories have a way of confirming just how beloved those persons are.

If I told you about my mother saying bedtime prayers with me in my upstairs bedroom at our old Arthur Street house in Atlanta, you might later remember what I told you—but not as I remember it. If I told you about going fishing with Pop and brother Walter on Saturday mornings in Tampa, you might later remember what I had told you—but not as I remember it.

(My brother John was too young for the fishing trips in those days. Oddly enough, he became the most avid fisherman in our family.) If I told you about meeting Keitha for the first time on the way to worship at our church in Miami, you might remember what I told you—but not as I remember it. If I told you about the first Christmas when we let Holly, our youngest, be the one to put the last figure in our now very old crèche, and she said as she put the Christ Child at the center, "Jesus is born!", you might remember what I told you—but not as I remember it. If I told you about how our eldest daughter recited with disbelief the exotic places where her classmates would be spending spring break, and how, when I asked her if she sometimes wished her parents had a lot of money, she answered without skipping a beat, "I like you just the way you are," you might remember what I told you—but not as Keitha and I remember it. The memories are precious because the persons are precious.

Our Christian faith is precious because it is completely wrapped up in Jesus. Not the Jesus of history, from whom we are far removed, but the living Jesus, now resurrected and through the Spirit available to us all. As we read the stories of Jesus in the Gospels, we are reading about the One who is now present with us. The memories of Jesus in the Gospel records are memories that become personal to us. In a very real sense, we are actually there. We are his students, we are those he heals, we are those he transforms. We remember as those who were there. And we must never forget that we were among those who betrayed him.

Prayer
Dear Jesus, today I give myself to you again. Help me to shape my life by what you tell me and show me in Scripture and not by my own cravings, fantasies, and pride. Please guide my life by the memory of your life. And grant me the empowering presence of your Holy Spirit to enable me to live as your transformed and recognizable disciple. Amen.

SATURDAY AFTER ASH WEDNESDAY
Memories of Jesus

Scripture for Reflection: The Four Gospels

Our memories help us understand ourselves. When our two daughters were teenagers, they sometimes asked Keitha what they were like as babies, every little detail. They wanted to be told what they couldn't consciously remember because in their infancy they didn't have words to construct the experience. They were looking for images of a story—*their* story.

An event of the past has meaning for us because of specific parts of the event that had an effect on us. For example, if you were to ask me what I remember about the few Winter Olympics I've watched I would say: It was the tears of Michelle Kwan. It was some teenage upstart named Tara Lipinski from Great Neck, New Jersey, giggling her way through something that was supposed to be so serious, as she blew us away with effortless twirls and breathtaking flights. (Her Gold Medal was anti-climactic.) It was Derek Parra, at the end of a race, looking up to the stands and saying to someone, "I love you." That's what I remember about those few Olympics games, and not much else.

What touches your heart and your mind from the life of Jesus? It's hard to answer that question if you are not acquainted with the four Gospels. Those Gospels are foundational for any follower of Jesus. They tell the actual *story* on which the rest of the New Testament depends. It makes no sense to have a belief in or a doctrine about Jesus if you have not actually met Jesus, studied him, or been deeply affected by his life. Otherwise you only have ideas and concepts which of themselves do not make you a Christian. You become a Christian when you give yourself to the *person* Jesus, and whereas you may start on your journey as a Christian knowing little about him, you must set yourself on a course to find out everything you can. (That is why all four Gospels were referenced at the beginning of this meditation.) Let your plea be expressed in the words of an old gospel song: "Tell me the story of Jesus, write on my heart every word."

It's the story we want, the story we need, the story that makes all the difference. Yes, we need sound doctrine about Jesus. Over the centuries, theologians have worked with diligence to define Jesus in doctrinal formulations as they aim to honor the astonishing unity of his humanity and his divinity. We do need the clarity they bring. But we must not assume that our intellectual belief in the doctrine is the same as our total commitment of our lives to the person.

We find the person—in person, if you like—in the Gospels. When we read the story of Jesus, we don't get every detail of his life—not everything he said, not everything he did. We get the memories of the witnesses and writers. We get what impacted and changed their lives. Three of the Gospel writers (Matthew, Mark, and Luke) follow a similar outline, yet each of them adds his own specific memories. John is different still, both in recalling some events not included in the other three and using a different choice of words intended to reach a different mindset.

When you become a reader of the Gospels, different parts of the story have special meaning and challenge for you at particular times in your life. When Jesus tells a parable about a good Samaritan, or one about a prodigal son, you may hear God prompting your heart toward some important change in a relationship. When you hear his radical teaching about how to live in the kingdom of God he is inaugurating, you may hear

God calling you to take some specific action immediately. When you see him freely and graciously forgiving this or that sinful person, you may hear God calling you to go and do likewise. When you see him suffering on a cruel cross, you may hear God saying, "This is how much I love you. Now what?"

In the life of Jesus, there is ever more to teach and transform us. Ever more to keep us focused on holy living. Ever more to draw us to the Throne of Grace, where we humble ourselves and seek enabling grace for this hour. We never outgrow our need for the Gospels, our Rule of Life, our New Testament Torah.

As we remember Jesus this Lenten season, let us ask ourselves how we can better let those Gospel memories shape our own lives. What difference does it make that at great risk, Jesus did the will of his Father in heaven, refused to compromise his calling, and loved us to death? And what does it say about where we go from here? Most importantly, how can our own memories bear some resemblance to what Jesus experienced, in the same way his first followers resembled him as their Rabbi and Lord?

Prayer
Dear Lord, I thank You for this opportunity to strengthen my memory of Jesus during this Lenten Season. I realize that my desire to be more like Jesus, more Christlike, rings hollow if I am not perfecting my memory of him. As I study Jesus during these days, help me to see clearly what he asks of me, his imitating disciple. And empower me, through Your Spirit, to live in such a way that others will see him in me. I pray this in his name, who lived and died for me. Amen.

SUNDAY THE FIRST WEEK OF LENT
Jesus Revealing Us

Scripture for Reflection: John 1:1-14; Matthew 11:25

A verse of a much revered and enduring Irish hymn is a good introduction to what our meditations will center on this week. The words are a love song and a prayer for a follower of Jesus:

> Be Thou my vision, O Lord of my heart!
> Naught be all else to me, save that Thou art;
> Thou my best thought, by day or by night,
> Waking or sleeping, Thy presence my light.

What do we mean when we sing such words? In what sense is our Lord Jesus our vision? How can we see through his eyes? Perhaps one of the reasons the Gospels were written was to help us see the difference between the ways Jesus saw particular people, situations, and events he encountered, and the ways his disciples did. Often, what he saw was not what they saw. They did not yet have Jesus' vision. One of Jesus' greatest challenges in discipling his Twelve was to get them to see the astonishing way he saw into people.

Jesus looked into a woman everyone knew was a sinner, and as she washed his feet and anointed his head with oil, he saw saving faith and deep love in her heart. He looked into a man who obeyed the commandments and seemed to have everything a person could want, and he saw the hollowness of a man who defined his worth by his possessions. He looked into a Samaritan woman with whom he was not supposed to have a conversation and had the conversation anyway—a deep and personal conversation—until she began to see herself as Jesus did. He encountered three men who claimed they really wanted to join Jesus' team, but Jesus saw their preferential conditions for a life he knew had to be completely unconditional. He looked into a seven-demon possessed woman, and he saw her into release and self-realization, a free woman who would follow him to his own death and beyond. He looked into the heart of a model pharisee, and he saw profound and desperate pride. He looked into the heart of another pharisee, and he saw the beginning of a journey into faith. Even from the cross, where he hung in undeserved, cruel punishment, he looked down and saw into those who didn't really know the gross injustice they were helping to carry out, and he asked his heavenly Father to forgive them.

What better Christians we would all be if, more and more, we had Jesus' eyesight! Resembling Jesus is a very difficult, in fact, impossible calling if we are not really interested in seeing how and what he sees. How could we love people as he did if we do not see deeper into their souls, their pain, their deep need, as he did—see beyond our own prejudices, stereotypes, and distastes?

We may see someone as a threat in some way because they have done something hurtful or demeaning toward us. Because the pain is still there, it blinds us and disables our ability to see the person Jesus sees. We remain blind to that person until the barrier of pain is crossed by reconciliation. We may be blinded to someone else because of our rigid stereotypes about people who are rich, or poor, or of a different race or ethnicity—you name the stereotype. Again, we remain blind to the person Jesus sees until the barrier of the stereotype is crossed by reaching across that barrier to risk exposure to the otherness that discomforts or threatens us. We may be blinded to seeing what Jesus sees in a person because the person's lifestyle and habits are so disgusting to us. And we remain blind to the person Jesus sees, until we can see and confess what we see disgusting in ourselves.

I'll never forget reading a quote from an early American Quaker who was an extremely devout Christian and active in the movement to eliminate slavery. This very holy man said that before he proceeded to pray for a person who was guilty of a certain sin, he would ask the Lord for forgiveness for that same sin in himself. It calls to mind Jesus' bold invitation to any member of a group of men blinded by their own self-righteousness to claim the right to throw the first stone based on his own sinlessness.

Jesus sees the good and the beautiful in people, but he sees the weaknesses and failures as well. Perhaps we can see as he does if we also are willing to see both the good and the bad. Seeing as Jesus sees can be hampered by our unwillingness to see the downside of a person. We may even go so far as to idolize someone, which is, as the term suggests, a form of idolatry. Idolizing someone makes of him or her an almost-perfect human being who seems to be immune to sin. In order to see a person that way, the idolizer would have to adopt a voluntary blindness and live in denial. Our seeing—and our relationship with that person for that matter—can be adversely affected by such fantasizing. When the idolized person finally shows he or she is a sinner, too, the idolizer is shattered and may even turn against the person. A healthy relationship requires both love and honesty.

Jesus does not ignore each person's sin. He sees it. He forgives it. But his vision sees through it till it reveals who the person was created and redeemed to become, and what steps need to be taken to move in that direction. Just imagine how good our spiritual vision would be if we saw through Jesus' eyes!

There is one more thing we dare not leave out in our pursuit of learning to see as Jesus sees. It's the matter of our eyes. What we see is interpreted through the filtering lens of our acquired learning, our set opinions, our good or bad fortunes, our belief system, and a variety of other influences. Jesus invites us to a different way of seeing. He reveals it in a prayer: "I praise you, Lord of heaven and earth, because you've hidden these things from the wise and intelligent and have shown them to babies" (Matthew 11:25). Earlier in the same chapter, he speaks of children in the marketplace calling out to others. They played the flute but no one danced, sang a funeral song and they didn't mourn (vv. 16-17). Later in Matthew's Gospel, Jesus says that to enter the kingdom of heaven, we must become like a child (18:3). Small children don't worry so much about their spin on what they see. They see as straight as they can.

Prayer
Dear Jesus, by your Holy Spirit enable me to see myself clearly through your eyes so that I can accept what is there and grow further by your grace. Help me to see others through your eyes, so that I can love them as they are and be you to them. And help me to see all of life through your eyes so that my witness can be reliable. Please be my vision, and your presence my light. Amen.

MONDAY THE FIRST WEEK OF LENT
Revealing Our Sin

Scripture for Reflection: Psalm 51

Jesus sees the best in us and the worst. The One who *is* the image of God sees we humans who were made *in* the image of God—for better and for worse. He sees when we resemble the image, and when we violate it.

This is very good news. It is good that he shows his love for us in both cases. When we violate the kind of person Jesus calls us to be—that is to say, when we sin—the love of God for us becomes a correcting love, a love that gives us a soulful sense that something we did or didn't do here does not fit who we are in Christ. On the other hand, when we are living in a way that does resemble Jesus, the love of God becomes an affirming love, a sense that we have tasted the kingdom of God and touched our true humanity.

How do we know, one way or another? We could mistake experiences that bring us good feelings for divine affirmation. For example, we may be attracted to doing good things for other people because it gives us an adrenalin rush of self-satisfaction, especially when what we do is recognized. Or we may do good to serve a hidden, self-serving end, perhaps to force the recipient of our kindness to be obligated to us. Along with this there are always those who are alert to recognize such imperfect motivations in others and find satisfaction and a sense of superiority in pointing out, or gossiping about, the do-gooder's *real* intent. I know all these tactics because I have been guilty of all of them. I'm especially good at the latter.

A goodly number of other Christians may be very accepting of their own sins, as if sinning were an unavoidably natural part of life on this earth. They recognize that they will never reach perfection in this life—which is true—and they then adopt a kind of resignation or even hopelessness about the possibility of making significant progress in Christlikeness. They may honestly confess their sins and seek forgiveness on a regular basis, but their disabling humility becomes a crutch of excuses, a justification of failure, and therefore a weakening of the will. The life Jesus taught, lived, and called his disciples to emulate is identified as an impossible ideal in this life, realistic only in heaven. (We could ask those who hold to that position, "Why would Jesus teach a way of life on earth that he knew his students would never be able to live on earth?")

Why does Jesus lovingly reveal our sins to us in the first place? Answer: to show us what needs fixing. Why does he lovingly affirm us when we live his way, in his image? Answer: to show us what doesn't need fixing, only further development. The key to all this is to *know* this Jesus, not a particular Jesus of our own making—and there are plenty of those around—but the Jesus we meet in the four Gospels. The minds of many of us in this world are full of fictional Jesuses, inventions to fit our purposes, accommodations to our wishes, intended or unintended heresies.

If you and I were made in the image of God, and if Jesus *is* that image of God and gave his life to enable us to recover the damaged image we now bear, then we must make it our personal mission to immerse ourselves in the four Gospels. We must seek Jesus on every page, open ourselves to what the words and sentences and stories reveal about him, even though it may not fit in with the views we are comfortable with. Otherwise, the Jesus we follow will be a fictional character.

As you read the Gospels this Lenten season, remember how Jesus looked into the face of those he met and knew the truth of what was there, the good and the bad, the holy and the unholy, the honest and the dishonest. Put yourself in each story and invite Jesus to turn his gaze on you, and then ask him what he sees. It may well lead you to make confession and to repent of a sin or a failure in his presence, where forgiveness is in more than sufficient supply. Or you may hear his "well done," followed by his encouragement to keep at it—or as Wesley would say, to "move on toward perfection." Thanks be to God!

Prayer
Dear heavenly Father, thank You for sending Jesus into our world to invite us and show us how to become our true selves. Dear Jesus, thank you for living as us and for us. Thank you for dying as you did and forgiving us as you have, so that we might live for you free of sin's dominion. I ask that you keep me honest about my faults and willing to confess my sins as your Holy Spirit so graciously enables me to do. I pray this through you, my Savior and Lord. Amen.

TUESDAY THE FIRST WEEK OF LENT
Revealing Our Forgiveness

Scripture for Reflection: Matthew 6:12;
Luke 6:37; Ephesians 4:32

Just about all of us know that Jesus expects us to forgive someone who has wronged us. It's tough to do. Not as many of us remember that the only way to do it—really do it—says Jesus, is to see ourselves as those who are never ourselves without the need for forgiveness. Being forgiven and giving forgiveness to others are both essential to who we are in Christ.

Come with me to the Jerusalem of Jesus' day, to old Mt. Moriah where the temple was built. The Southern Steps outside the temple were known as the Teaching Steps. The rabbis would gather there to teach their disciples and anyone else who would listen. Jesus was one of those rabbis, and here his teachings engaged more directly with issues of Jewish law. Let's consider one of those teaching moments.

A group of pharisees and Jewish theologians bring a high-profile case (John 8:1-11). They want to trap Jesus into not honoring the Law handed down from Moses. They present a woman caught in adultery. The Law, they say, says that she must be stoned—never mind that the Law says both parties to the sin must be put to death, also that the sentence of stoning is limited to cases of adultery where the woman is a virgin betrothed to another man. Jesus, however, doesn't seem interested in getting into details of the Law. He doesn't approach this situation as a legal case. His focus is on the woman before him who *knows* that she is broken, and on the accusing pharisees and theologians who *don't* know they are, too.

The problem here is that a sinful woman is being judged by men who are using their publicly profiled righteousness to hide their own sin. Just their lust for trapping Jesus and then being able to damage his public profile as a respected rabbi are sin enough to question their right to judge.

We have no record of what Jesus wrote as he paused to carve words into the dirt. What we do know is what he says: "Whoever hasn't sinned should throw the first stone." What we do know is that in one sentence Jesus delivers a sermon for every one of us. (This is where the accusers depart quietly.) It's not that the Law and our Christian ethics aren't important. They are. Jesus teaches us to pray that God's will be done on earth as it is in heaven, and he expects that we pursue purity of heart and holiness of life. Let us not forget that he also says that every time we pray, we must ask for the Father's forgiveness of our *own* transgressions.

The Lord's prayer doesn't even stop there. Jesus also says that the Lord's forgiveness of us will have no effect unless we forgive others. "Forgive us of the ways we have wronged you, *just as we also forgive* those who have wronged us" (italics added). Forgiveness is a two-way street. We cannot ask and receive forgiveness from God for our own sins unless we are ready to forgive those who have wronged us or violated the standards of our faith. Forgiveness opens our hearts and makes us forgiving persons. That is beyond the grasp of those who deny their need for forgiveness and are intolerant of the sins of others.

Jesus sets us free from all that. He refuses to debate over what the Law says the woman deserves. He drops the case and looks into the woman's face. "Woman," he says, "where are they? Does no one now condemn you?" "No one, sir," she replies. "Then neither do I condemn you. Go now and leave your life of sin." Forgiveness followed by empowerment.

Three Greek words in the New Testament are usually translated "forgive." Two of them have the sense of releasing or setting someone free, leaving something behind. No groveling. The other is a verb based on the word that means "grace." In Luke 7:41-43, Jesus uses this word to teach Peter that the greater the debt forgiven, the greater the grace received. In Ephesians 4:32 and Colossians 3:13, Paul invites us to take the grace of Christ's forgiveness of us and turn it into the grace of forgiving each other. In Christ we are called to be forgivers of even those who are the most difficult to forgive. Such is our way of life in Christ.

What a crazy way to live! No tit for tat. No getting even. No dishing out deserved retribution. Just the freedom—and the discipline—of living a gracious, forgiving, Christlike life.

Prayer
Heavenly Father, there's no one but Jesus who has walked this earth teaching us by his own life to embody forgiveness in the way we live and love, and to release others from our self-righteous condemnation of them. Lord, rob us of our spiritual smugness so that we can be in a state of heart to receive, and give, forgiveness. We ask this in the name of the One who so fully embodied forgiveness, the one who hung on a cruel cross, with every reason to condemn us all, and cried out instead, "Father, forgive them!" Amen.

WEDNESDAY THE FIRST WEEK OF LENT
Revealing Our Homelessness

Scripture for Reflection: Luke 9:57-62

I was moved by a documentary about a homeless woman named Linda. It was entitled "God Knows Where I Am." For most of her years, she lived a normal life. Considered a happy person by her family and friends, she held down good jobs. In her middle years, however, her behavior began to change when her love fantasies centered around a certain man, and over time it became clear that nothing was going to come of the relationship. She became psychotic and spent time in hospitals for treatment. She was released a few times when doctors considered her well enough to cope.

The last time she was released she became homeless. Even her sister didn't know where she was. Linda eventually found an abandoned house within sight of a two-lane highway, not far from her hometown in New England where the sister lived. In fact, her sister drove that highway almost every day, not knowing that a place she could see from the highway was where Linda was living. In all her efforts to find Linda, she had failed. In fact, no one knew that someone was living in that old house.

Linda survived in her home well over a year, as her decline into psychosis continued. She lived almost entirely on apples from the abandoned orchard next to the house. The old heating system was inoperative, so her decline was hastened by the cold New England winter days. She kept a daily journal, a record of her gradual regression. A few days before she finally succumbed to the cold, she wrote in the journal, "God knows where I am." God was the only one.

Linda's story parallels the story of a world of homeless people who have lost rootedness and relationships. They are the tens of thousands of people who sleep on the streets in nations both poor and rich, and people from nations where it is too dangerous for a family to live, now on the border of nations too difficult to enter. They are also people living a seemingly normal life in a Western nation while deep inside they feel disconnected from home—by distance in this highly mobile world, by a family that spends very little time together, by a busyness that prevents deeper conversations, by a deep sense of alienation, or by some other personal suffering they don't know how to share.

The search for home is nothing new in the history of our race. One could look at the whole Biblical story as a search for home. It begins in Genesis where God creates both a human race of two people that need each other and a Garden as their home. Their sin puts a barrier between them (Genesis 3:15) and robs them of their home (3:21-24). Their descendants fail again and again to escape the sin and to establish a lasting home. Along comes Jesus, one of their very own, a homeless man himself. He offers, not a homeland on this earth but a homeland of the heart. He gathers around him a new kind of family that shares his forgiveness, his holy way of living, his love for God and one another. It's a kind of family that can be formed in any place and with any race. It is transportable, inclusive, and hospitable. And as long as this family follows its Founder, it will be a place to call home.

Linda's homelessness was an extremity brought on by psychotic decline; in the end, she could no longer relate to people. Each of the homeless people who comes to my Salvation Army church during the week for food, a shower, a meal, and needed referrals has a different story. Some of them have been homeless for so long it seems they are trapped for life, as if homelessness were their life's assignment.

There is yet another kind of homelessness, a hidden homelessness. The fractured family, the constant changes and mobilities that cut off enduring relationships, the fake friendships made for an advantage, and the general loss of community that is eroding the very fabric of our society—these have spawned a civilization of more homeless people than we see on the street or in an old abandoned house somewhere. Their destitution is of the heart. They feel alienated from those around them, even though they may be "functioning" well enough. They are the hidden homeless though they are many.

Jesus was a homeless man (Luke 9:58) who carried home with him. His invitations were to join a family without physical or ancestral boundaries. To the homeless demented man of Gerasa he brought a holy sanity and restored him to his hometown family (Mark 5:1-20). To a tax collector named Matthew he brought membership in a small but growing family that offered inclusion rather than exploitation (Mark 2:13-17). To a rich man he offered the opportunity to join the human family by giving his wealth to the poor (Luke 18:18-23). To us all, Jesus offers us his body broken, the supreme revelation of his saving love, and with it comes membership in his family, a taste on earth of our eternal Home.

Prayer
Loving God, I thank you that in a fractured world such as ours, you sent Jesus to rescue us from the curse of all forms of homelessness. I confess whatever brokenness may still resides in my own heart and my failures sometimes to bring relational healing. Please help me to be sensitive to the pain of the homeless. I ask this in the name of Jesus, who had nowhere to lay his head. Amen.

THURSDAY THE FIRST WEEK OF LENT
Revealing Our Community

Scripture for Reflection: Genesis 2:18, 21-25

The cure for homelessness is community. God—who is a Community of Father, Son, and Holy Spirit—is not a loner, and He did not create us as loners. It never was, and still isn't, good for any of us to be alone (Genesis 2:18a). Linda's isolation from others would inevitably lead to her death (previous meditation).

The creation of the second human marks the beginning of community, and from there on we live in groups large and small. Our English word "community" is taken from an older word that meant "common," not common in the sense of low-class, mediocre, run-of-the-mill, or vulgar, but common in the sense of what we share together as humans, what unites us, what marks us all as humans created in God's image. In the truest sense of the word, a community values each of its members equally, does not allow the demeaning of any member, and opens membership to anyone who will value other members in the same way. If any of this seems familiar, it's probably because it sounds suspiciously like some of the things Jesus and other New Testament writers say about the church, the community of Jesus' followers.

The New Testament Greek word *koinonia* is even more helpful. Used to describe the church, it is usually translated "fellowship," and the meaning includes "a close mutual relationship; participation, sharing in; partnership; contribution; gift." In the form of an adjective, the meaning is "generous" or "liberal." In Acts 2:42, the early church is described as a fellowship of sharing; in I Corinthians 1:9 as the fellowship of the Son; in Philippians 1:5 as a fellowship in gospel partnership; in Philippians 2:1 as a fellowship in the Spirit; in Philippians 3:10 as the fellowship of Jesus' sufferings; in I John 1:3 as a fellowship with the Father and his Son; in I John 1:7 as the fellowship of those who walk in the light.

Why is it important to understand what the New Testament means by the community of Jesus' followers? All too often the church or a church bears little resemblance to the scriptural descriptions cited in the previous paragraph. Some congregations are rife with one, some, or all exhibiting divisiveness, status seeking, powering mongering, position grabbing. Others pursue obsessive concerns over matters of insignificance, complex procedure, minute details, or hollow rituals. Still others have an unholy settledness and a stubborn resistance to change. All these dysfunctions can continue to exist in the church if we allow them to. Or we can confess our sins against our Lord and his Body, repent, and start changing.

I'm struck—and largely convinced—by Frank Buechner's impression of most churches he's been to as less like church than the AA groups he's visited and the Adult Children of Alcoholics group he's a member of, where people are accepted, honesty reigns, and even the confrontations are acts of love.

The true church is a *koinonia* community. It is not defined as an appropriately attractive structure where we gather for corporate worship. It is a group of fellow believers we join with, once, twice, or more times during the week. They may meet in an attractive building or a decrepit old structure or in no building at all. And if the number of worshipers is large, these same believers also meet in smaller groups for spiritual intimacy and accountability.

The true church is like a really good family gathering, like a family meal that is so much more than most family meals because transformation happens as the family gathers in love and prays in unity. At this gathering Jesus gives us his body, broken, and sacrificed for us. He shares the cup of his covenant, his saving blood poured out over the whole dying world. Here we become one community in Christ, founded by a cross, a resurrection, and a Holy Spirit Pentecost—a community transformed by incomprehensible love. Here, there is no such thing as a homeless person.

Prayer

Dear Lord, we confess that sometimes, or perhaps often, our church bears little resemblance to the Body of Christ, to the community that Jesus gave his life to make possible. Please sanctify me, and sanctify the congregation I belong to, so that I can do my part, and all of us can come together to be who and what you want us to be as your church. I pray this in the name of Jesus, who gifted us with each other. Amen.

FRIDAY THE FIRST WEEK OF LENT
Revealing Our Mission

Scripture for Reflection: Acts 1:1-8

Some churches have little or no sense of mission. Their members come to church for other reasons, most of them having to do with habit, self-interest, respectability, or long-term family ties. Maybe some are searching for meaning in life, and they haven't yet found it, though they keep hoping. In each case their church's mission in the world, if it exists at all, is carried out as obligatory duty.

Some churches think mission is something a church *does*, a commendable activity, perhaps a service to the needy. The shocking thing we find in Scripture is that mission is actually what the church *is*. This community we talked about in yesterday's meditation is *a community in mission*. When Jesus sends out his disciples for the last time in Acts 1:1-8, he says nothing about the church itself and certainly nothing about how to run a church. The calling he gives those now eleven disciples does not require skills learned at a seminary. They are to expect a baptism with the Holy Spirit, soon to come, and then they will be Jesus' *witnesses* "in Jerusalem, in all Judea and Samaria, and to the end of the earth" (v. 8). In those days those places named meant the whole of the human race. The baptism came on Pentecost (chapter 2), and the Christian movement exploded (vv. 42-47).

How did it happen? It happened because those first Christians understood what that word "witnesses" meant, and they embraced it. The Greek word meant "testimony, witness; evidence, proof; reputation." Throw all those meanings together and you get a description of what our calling to be an authentic witness to the gospel looks like. It means living a life that is a testimony to our belief in the person Jesus as the Savior for all humankind. It means giving credible evidence that Jesus is, in fact, the model after whom we are patterning our lives. And it means we are getting a reputation as so committed to Jesus that we would rather die than deny him. (Incidentally, the same Greek word was used to form an English word: martyr—the ultimate witness!)

Our resurrected Lord charges his disciples to proclaim the good news and bring people to faith (Mark 16:15; Luke 24:47), proclaim the forgiveness of sins (John 20:21-23), and make and mold disciples wherever we are in this world (Matthew 28:16-20). How is this to be done? Obviously by proclamation of the gospel, followed by discipling. This calling falls on its face, no matter how well done, if the living of Christians does not credibly match the message preached. When the two don't merge, ours is a paper gospel, a set of beliefs that fail to touch the heart, only the mind. It is a Christianity without a valid witness. In our day, the church has not so much failed in its preaching as in its validating evidence.

Our mission is to be Jesus in the world in which we live. As the people of Israel were called to be a blessing to the nations, so the church is called to proclaim that this blessing has "come through Christ Jesus and…the promise of the Spirit through faith" (Galatians 3:14). How well is your congregation doing in blessing those who are not its members? How well are *you* doing? Jesus calls all who would follow him to suffer persecution for his sake (Matthew 5:38-42) and love their enemies (5:43-44). In this world where hatred of certain groups—social, racial, political, and religious—is considered justifiable by many Christians, how well are you following Jesus' clear commands to the contrary?

There is nothing that could better turn around a congregation that is self-centered and suffocating spiritually than for the Spirit of God to give them this: a holiness that redirects them to the world that God loves and for which Jesus died, where they can find their calling as compassionate witnesses.

Prayer
Dear Jesus, whose painful and loving relationship with this sinful world brought you to a cross, I want my love for you to possess me and propel me to be your witness every day I live, wherever I am and no matter how threatening the situation. Please grant me this request and send me the enabling gift of your Holy Spirit. Amen.

SATURDAY THE FIRST WEEK OF LENT
Revealing Our Future

Scripture for Reflection: Revelation 21:1-7

The Bible is a book that looks to the future. The Old Testament is saturated with the promise of a better tomorrow for God's people. Prophets like Isaiah strain toward a day when the brokenness of nations and the sin of the human heart will be healed (Isaiah, chapters 55 and 56). At a very difficult time when the Babylonian army has surrounded Jerusalem and defeat is imminent, Jeremiah believes God will once again bring blessing and prosperity, and to prove his belief he purchases a field. He makes an investment in the land at precisely the moment it is about to be lost (Jeremiah, chapter 32). The Old Testament ends with words about a new future. Malachi speaks of God sending a messenger, a second Elijah, who will refine the nation with fire, a sun of righteousness who will bring healing to those revering God's name (Malachi 3:1-3, chapter 4). The reader is left looking to that future.

In the Gospels Jesus calls this future "the kingdom of God." He says that it has now come. "If I throw out demons by the power of God," he proclaims, "then God's kingdom has already overtaken you" (Luke 11:20). The apostle Paul affirms that through Christ "God was reconciling the world to Himself" (II Corinthians 5:19). Even though the kingdom had come in Jesus, however, it had not yet reached its fullness. For this reason, Jesus' followers are commanded by their resurrected Lord to go into the world and bring others to faith (Luke 24:47; Matthew 28:18-20). In other words, you and I have an important role to play in bringing in God's future.

How do we do this? The best answer to that question, I believe, is this: We live our lives in ways that point to that future. We speak the good news, to be sure, but it is our lives, not so much our claims, that will convince others that the kingdom of God *is* the future.

At one time in the Western world, most people claimed to be Christians, but many were not living as if they were. Christian faith was little more than a part of one's cultural identity. In such a world, evangelism was a call to a genuine conversion to the radical way of life taught by Jesus. Jesus was more than the Savior who forgave their sins; he was also the model for living in God's kingdom. Those who moved beyond a name-only Christianity and started taking the kingdom Jesus taught seriously often found themselves in conflict with the dominant values of the culture in which they lived. Sometimes they suffered for it, as Christians always have; and sometimes their authenticity and courage drew others to deeper faith.

In our day, less and less can we assume we are witnessing to people who already believe in Christ or even have a Christian background of any kind. They may have no predispositions toward Jesus—and they may distinctly *not* believe in the validity of the Christian religion. They may have seen too many shallow, compromising Christians and heard of too many televangelists building personal empires through their version of Christianity. Such people cannot be argued into faith or convinced by a flood of Bible verses. They can, however, be won over by Christians who bear resemblance to Jesus, the image of God in human flesh. They can be convinced by Christians who manifest the compassion and joy of their faith. They can be convinced by authentic holy living. It is our allegiance to Christ and our likeness to him that will stun the world and capture the heart. This is our calling.

In accepting such a calling, we can be assured that God is with us. We call it His providence. He will never leave us or forsake us. Bad things can happen to us because we are witnesses, and witnesses take risks. Providence is not protection; it is provision. For Jesus' witnesses, all things, including the bad things, work together for good (Romans 8:28). The witness endures, even though our earthly lives, fragile as they are, may not. Jeremiah-like, we risk investing ourselves in God's future.

It takes courage to live the future in the present. It takes strength to refuse naked self-interest and adopt the giving life of God's coming kingdom. It takes holy confidence to live the life of Jesus today when it so often means being unusual, and even odd. It takes disciples who see the future and know it is in God's hands, disciples who live that future because they know it is really the only way worth living.

So like Peter, we rejoice in hope even though it brings trials. Through our tested faith we glorify and honor Jesus, whom we love and trust even without seeing him. We rejoice with glorious joy, too great to put into words. All the while we are receiving the goal of our faith: our salvation (I Peter 1:6-9).

Prayer

Dear God, I thank you that you have my best interests at heart. Help me to see that what may seem best for me may not be. Give me the courage to live by the values and behaviors of the kingdom of God, even when it may embarrass me or cause me trouble. If I compromise my calling, please recall me for correction. If I fail to trust you, let me learn from the failure that follows. If I pretend holiness, please embarrass me by my own fakery. If I question the future of "a new heaven and a new earth," help me see the vision of Jesus becoming reality in people's lives. I ask this in his name. Amen.

SUNDAY THE SECOND WEEK OF LENT
Jesus Humbling Us

Scripture for Reflection: Isaiah 66:2b;
John 13:16; James 4:10; I Peter 5:5b-6

When we read the above Scripture verses, it becomes clear that the eyes of God look to the humble and contrite in spirit and that all disciples of Jesus are called to clothe themselves with humility. Contrary to our way of thinking, the one who sends us into the world to represent him is not someone who revels in his authority as our regal sender. He actually claims to be "gentle and humble in heart" himself (Matthew 11:29b, NIV). As we read through Scripture, we begin to see that humility is what God is looking for in all of us—and in Jesus, we see it in full view. None of us is called not to be humble. Humility is the doorway to our true humanity (our holiness).

The truly humble people I've had the privilege to know over my lifetime have both shamed me for my presumption and helped me by their influence. I'm especially thinking now of Harold Hill. I made his acquaintance in the mid-1960s. He was a university student in New Zealand, and I was a seminary student in the USA. We both were lay members of The Salvation Army (Salvationists) and were involved in publishing, along with others, our own independent journals for Salvationists in our respective countries who wanted to bring change in our denomination. We corresponded by international snail mail (long distance phone calls were too expensive). We shared ideas and one another's articles. In a way, we were co-conspirators.

Our paths were both similar and different. Harold and his wife, Pat, became Salvation Army officers and spent much of their calling serving in Third World countries. I and my wife, Keitha, also became Salvation Army officers and, save for brief seminars and conferences in Third World countries and Europe, spent our calling in the USA and Great Britain. Harold and Pat's preference for serving in countries where poverty was rampant says something telling about them: They weren't aiming at organizational advancement; they were looking for how they could best serve those considered the least, the ones with whom Jesus spent most of his time, the ones our denomination came into being to serve. I hardly knew Pat, and my encounters with Harold were very few and far between. I knew him mostly through occasional correspondence and his superb writings. He combined quiet humility, courageous thinking, and penetrating wit. His modesty was as disarming as his searing intellect. Through his life and writings, he called The Salvation Army to never forget her roots. The Salvation Army's main denominational publication in New Zealand carried his obituary soon after he died. His photo on the cover dominated the page. It was labeled with these words: "A Dangerous Salvationist." What a tribute to the hidden and authentic power of the humble!

Humility is too often identified with weakness when it is, in fact, the greatest strength. It is the greatest strength because it is the gift of the greatest love. Humility is not a condition one is forced into—like poverty, or being a victim of racial discrimination, or having low self-esteem because of abuse. Humility is a conscious choice to live out of a deep inner life rather than a prosperous exterior life. The exterior life is important to the humble, but primarily as the place of loving God and others, as the place of unselfish service, as the place to follow Jesus. The humble live well in the world as credible followers of Jesus *because* of the depth of their inner life with God. Their great strength, as Howard Thurman has taught us, is that their inner life, their soul, is the one thing those who seek dominance cannot possess. The truly humble cannot be humiliated (*Jesus and the Disinherited*). The humble are the bravest people on the planet because they, like their Lord, have died to themselves (Luke 9:23-24).

Some may look upon humility as unhealthy. They say, rather, that it's healthy to have a strong sense of self-worth, a confident self-image, a clear sense of one's self-identity. The irony is that this is precisely what the humble *do* have. They know who they are in Christ, and who they are not. Humility is not self-denigration; it is self-acceptance. The humble do not seek to build a reputation; their lives are their reputation. Those whose sense of self-worth is something which they have to prove, their self-image something they have to work to promote, their self-identity something they have to create, are desperate. The truly humble need none of this. They are the healthy ones.

An interesting study conducted at Pepperdine University sought to measure "intellectual humility," which was defined as an awareness of those participating of how incomplete and fallible were their views on political and social issues. Those who scored high on intellectual humility also scored lower on political and ideological polarization, whether conservative or liberal. They were less aggressive and less judgmental toward members of other religious groups, and they were not easily manipulated with regard to their own views (*The Atlanta Journal-Constitution*, "Healthy humility has roots in curiosity, reflection," 11/17/19, p. E5). Now "intellectual humility" is not the same as the more deeply spiritual humility that we are dealing with in this meditation. But I suspect there is some correlation. Truly humble followers of Jesus understand that polarization is not his way; reconciliation is. Arguments and intellectual battles will not win anyone to Christian faith. Embodying the powerful humility of Jesus will.

Writer Flannery O'Conner believed that humility requires a willingness to live in or with *mystery*. "Mystery," she said, "is a great embarrassment to the modern mind." If something can't be analyzed, organized, quantified, theorized, utilized, or exploited, for many it doesn't exist. It can't be seriously considered. It's useless.

We live in this world of exploitation. People exploit each other and their planet. Even the church can become a place for self-promotion or earthly empire-building, as the mystery of grace and the power of humble love are trampled in the stampede of grasping benefits. Some churches have become one-stop service centers, with enough programs to meet any need, drawing people by the variety of services offered and the solutions promised. These can be a very helpful part of a congregation's ministry. The danger is that the congregation may get so caught up in the attractiveness and practicalities of the programs that the cultivation of the divine mystery into which Jesus calls his people is lost, as is the humility that it cultivates in us.

The Letter of James says, "Humble yourselves before the Lord, and he will lift you up" (4:10). We don't need to lift ourselves up; the Lord does that. We need to humble ourselves into our utter need of God, his Son, and the Holy Spirit, and then trust them to fill us with love and make grace the environment in which we live.

This week, we will explore six ways Jesus humbles us into likeness to Jesus. Perhaps the following prayer will help at the beginning of the journey.

Prayer

Humble Savior, as I embark on this journey toward Christlike humility, please give me discernment of my true motives, strength to confess my shortcomings and sin, and courage to trust the power of love and reject the pursuit of self-promotion. I ask this in your Name. Amen.

MONDAY THE SECOND WEEK OF LENT
Seeing the Nothings

Scripture for Reflection: Romans 8:26-32; I John 1:5-10

> Our worst fear is discovering that there is nothing at the center of who we are; a nothingness that is concealed only by avoidance and the distractions that we find for ourselves. Spiritual growth begins when we dare to peer into the nothing and find God peering back at us (*Celtic Daily Prayer: Book Two—Farther Up and Farther In*, p. 1360).

We can move forward on our spiritual journey when we're willing to hear God tell us that what we may have thought were our somethings are actually our nothings. We all have our somethings that prove to be nothings. It may be an endeavor that has absorbed us—perhaps for years—and we discover it is only a distraction, a nothing, an escape from a something worthwhile. Or it may be a source of pleasure we come to admit is no longer satisfying; perhaps it is even demeaning. It may be a direction our lives have taken, and we realize fulfillment isn't there. Maybe we've thought about how we've lived as a Christian and have come to suspect we've missed the heart of what it means to follow Jesus.

The God who created us made us in his image. That is our true something; that is who we are. The story of our fall from grace, told with such poignancy in Genesis, is the story of every one of us. It is the story of humans trading their identity as worshipers of God alone for an identity as worshipers of themselves. The snake in Eden's garden represents this lie, and Adam and Eve represent us all, the human race deceived and deluded. What follows is a history of humans reconstructing themselves out of nothings, out of a narrative of lies. Jesus' mission was to expose the lie and become for us the truth, the way to it, and the life of it lived (John 14:6). He came to save his people from their sins (Matthew 1:21) and their delusions (John 8:32).

When we humble ourselves before God and listen with faith and openness, he will help us see through our false somethings (the nothings). He puts his finger on something in our lives and tells us, "This something of yours has no substance, no reality, no future. It will turn to dust just as your earthly body will."

All nothings begin with somethings. The somethings are God's gifts to us; the nothings are abuses of those gifts. When we abuse God's gifts, we abuse Him, ourselves, and others. When we trash this earth He created, we insult him and our fellow humans for whom He created it. When we surrender the enlightened freedom we have in Christ to the agenda and tactics of any political party, we degrade that freedom. When we take our precious life and misuse it through unhealthy habits or self-serving ends, we are abusing God's gift. When we fail to invest in our marriages and take our marriage partner for granted, we are abusing God's gift. When we treat our parents, our children, or our friends with disdain, we are abusing God's gift. When we turn our occupation into an obsession to succeed over others and advance ourselves, we are abusing our calling to serve others. In all these and other cases, we are taking something precious that God has given us and making it into a nothing. We are degrading our true humanity. We are sinning. We are making nothings out of our God-given somethings.

Any of these abuses can emerge so innocently and develop so gradually that we are not aware of them, and, when they become established patterns, they are powerful forces against our holy humanity. One of C. S. Lewis's classics is about advice senior devil Screwtape gives to his apprentice devil Wormwood. He tells Wormwood to forget about tempting his victim with spectacular, high-impact sin. Here instead is his sage advice: "...the safest road to Hell is the gradual one—the gentle slope, soft-underfoot, without sudden turnings, without milestones, without signposts" (*The Screwtape Letters*). The earlier we can see that we are beginning to turn God's gift into a nothing, the better our position to repent and begin again.

Every follower of Jesus does well to look closely at himself and ask if he is honoring the gifts God has given him. It is, indeed, a humbling risk to bare our souls, to examine our hearts, to measure the real substance of our lives. It requires us to leave behind our pretenses and subtle lies, perhaps even the "high esteem" in which we are held by others. To what end? To see ourselves clearly in the gaze of a God who loves us more than we can imagine and who invites us, in His strength, to confess our abuse of His gifts, and then, by His enabling grace, to begin again. It's as if we are looking into a mirror and seeing Jesus, the very image of God, and through the Spirit allowing ourselves to be "transformed into that same image from one degree of glory to the next degree" (II Corinthians 3:18). A work of grace has begun.

Prayer

Heavenly Father, thank you for creating us in Your image and trusting us with it. I confess that I have abused that image by my sin. Even now, having come to faith, I still fall short and need to confess my sins. Help me to see ways I can turn my nothings into Your somethings, or my pride into a genuine humbling before You and others, or my divided loyalties into wholeness of life in Jesus. I ask this in his name, Amen.

TUESDAY THE SECOND WEEK OF LENT
Claiming the Real Somethings

Scripture for Reflection: Luke 5:27-32;
II Corinthians 7:8-11; II Peter 3:8-9

Yesterday we prayed for the honesty to see ourselves as we are. We looked at our pretenses and our delusions about ourselves. We considered our accomplishments, our self-made somethings, and challenged ourselves to ask whether they may really be nothings. We do this without fear because we do it in the presence of Christ. He humbles us with no interest in demeaning us. He only wants us to see where we are and to bring us to who we can be in God's image.

Once we discover and confess where we are, we are ready to repent. The New Testament Greek word that has traditionally been translated as "repent" means more than being sorry for our sins. It means "a change of heart, a turning from our sins, a change of our way or direction."

So, what stands in the way of this change of heart? Well for one thing, it's our ego, something we all have. Our ego gives us confidence—or maybe it tries to hide our lack of self-confidence by pretending. We insist we're doing well as Christians; we do a lot of good things. Certainly, God loves us for it. Does he? "But when God our savior's kindness and love appeared, he saved us because of his mercy, not because of righteous things we had done" (Titus 3:5a). Lines from a hymn of Augustus Toplady describe the reality well: "Nothing in my hands I bring,/ Simply to Thy cross I cling;/ Naked, come to Thee for dress,/ Helpless, look to Thee for grace" ("Rock of Ages," v. 3). Repentance starts with humbling ourselves in the presence of Christ in preparation for the radical change he is ready to make in our lives.

The humbling may require repenting of our acceptance of the shallow Christianity which is suffusing the airways and media—hucksters selling an easy faith with little or no heart change but plenty of painless righteousness and earthly rewards. Or it may require repenting of an all-too quiet and timid Christian life, a Christianity contained and cozy—and therefore ineffective in furthering the cause of Christ. Or it may be repenting of a Christian life lived for the purpose of advancing our respect, regard, influence, and even power in the church or in the world—a Christianity insidiously used to advance a hidden personal agenda. Or it may be something else still…

Catherine Booth (Co-Founder of The Salvation Army) grieved over what she saw as an overwhelming number of superficial conversions to Christ. "We should not only ask are people converted," she writes, "but what are they converted to? What sort of saints are they?…you had far better let a man alone in sin than give him a sham conversion and make him believe he is a Christian when he is nothing of the kind" (*Through the Year with Catherine Booth*, p. 102). Catherine does not mince words, nor should we deny the reality of a Christian church that is far too settled, self-serving, and safe because it is populated by Christians who have set comfortable boundaries for how far they will allow the love of Christ to take them. I know because I have been one of them.

True repentance is confession of and sorrow for our sins. And it is far more. It is an upheaval of our heart. It is a humbling of our closed mind and narrow vision, and a stark change in how we live our lives in the world. It is a lowering of ourselves as Christ lowered himself so that we can see the world through his eyes and give ourselves to its salvation as he did. At his hearing before Agrippa, the apostle Paul summed it up this way: "My message was that that they should change their hearts and lives and turn to God, and that they should demonstrate this change in their behavior" (Acts 26:20).

The changing progresses over a lifetime. Our conversion is not the end; it is the beginning. The Christian life is a journey with ever new discoveries and deeper "conversions" as we follow Jesus and are led by his Spirit to another holy something in his image to be claimed in the place of our nothing.

Prayer
Dear Jesus, humble Savior and Revealer, please keep me on the path of a lowly learner and a growing saint. Give me the courage to surrender my nothings for the deeper, more transformative gifts of likeness to you. I ask this in your strong name. Amen.

WEDNESDAY THE SECOND WEEK OF LENT
Beginning Again

Scripture for Reflection: Philippians, chapter 3

A person's claim to be humble always falls flat. The very claim belies itself. Someone might say you are humble, but if *you* claim it, your credibility is down the drain. I can't think of anyone in the New Testament who claimed to be humble, save Jesus (Matthew 11:29b), who was the full embodiment of humble, holy humanity. He needed no makeovers, only opportunities to live his humanity before us.

We have no right to claim humility. What we can and ought to claim is our *humbling*. How is it even possible to hear the words or the story of Jesus and not be humbled? How is it possible to observe the life of a fellow Christian whose Christlikeness in some area far exceeds our own and not be humbled? God has given us Scripture and the examples of other Christians in order to humble us. Sometimes we observe the behavior of a person who believes and practices a different religion, or no religion, and we are humbled because in some way they are more Christlike than we are.

Humbling is good. It is not a demeaning; it is a door to spiritual growth. It is something that happens to us that opens our hearts to being better disciples of Jesus. It is God making us aware of a dimension of holy living that it is time for us to enter. Maybe we see something or someone that helps us become aware of the possibility of greater Christlikeness. The seeing humbles us. A door to new grace in our lives is opened, grace to empower us to be more like Jesus. To be humbled is not to be diminished, but enlarged; not to be humiliated, but uplifted;

not to be embarrassed, but enlightened; not to be exposed, but re-clothed; not to be immobilized, but empowered.

To put it briefly, to be humbled is to free ourselves to be in a place where we're ready to allow Christ to change us for the better in some new way. The humbling reveals a nothingness in our lives that grace wants to fill with a holy something. Receiving the humbling creates a receptiveness to this new thing God is pleased to give us. No humbling, no real growth. The apostle Paul knew this well, as we see in the third chapter of his letter to the church at Philippi. Those things he had considered as assets in his life have now become nothings, as he moves toward the ultimate goal: "the prize of God's upward call in Christ Jesus."

We become Christians when we confess our sins and allow Jesus to change our hearts and lives, and when we then pledge to follow him all the days of our lives. This is the launching of our Christian journey. We find, however, that the journey is a spiritual learning track, and the learning is a matter of the heart more than the head, the living more the point than the thinking. The first Spirit-inspired challenge of the apostle Peter to those gathered at Pentecost, who now want to know what they should do following the outpouring, is simply this: "Change your hearts and lives." How this happens is through baptism (conversion to and by Christ) and receiving the enabling, purifying gift of the Holy Spirit (Acts 2:37-38). The mind follows the heart and what it learns from Christ-led living. Our minds can learn and recite correct Christian doctrines, but God looks at the heart and life. Theologians and denominations differ about details of doctrines, but God looks at the heart. Yes, we should strive to confess beliefs that as best we know are consistent with Scripture—given that we *do*, in fact, read, study, and pray over Scripture! But at the end of the day, God looks at the heart and the life.

A healthy, growing Christian life is filled with humblings followed by new beginnings. These new beginnings do not replace our conversion to Christ, they deepen it and often expand it. Our growth in grace is not so much a straight line as a series of revelations or convictions followed by humblings, which lead to new changes. It's like a couple who have become husband and wife making positive changes over the course of their married life, each change like a new conversion or a return to an earlier change that had been lost. Readers who are married will remember that most of those marital conversions required a humbling of some sort and often a confession. The willingness to be humbled is as essential to an authentic Christian life as it is to a healthy married life, or any enduring friendship for that matter.

I write this as someone who finally gave up his perfectionist illusions and realized that his life with God and others is a journey marked by humblings and followed, sooner or later, with new beginnings. Christ invites us all to humble ourselves so that we can begin again.

Prayer
Dear Jesus, I confess that I have sometimes been captive to my self-satisfaction and resistant to the change you want to make in my life at this time. Please strengthen my willingness to be humbled by you. Weaken my opposition to the change. And in the humbling may I find new insight into how I can more genuinely be like you and love like you. I pray this in your name. Amen.

THURSDAY THE SECOND WEEK OF LENT
Trusting

Scripture for Reflection: Psalm 121; John 16:29-33

Most of 2020 during the COVID-19 outbreak, we self-quarantined in our little mountain cabin. Because of our advanced years, the medical experts say we are more likely to die if we are infected by this aggressive virus. The reality of our vulnerability has given us pause. Life is more fragile than we may have thought.

On a day in early May of this year, I wrote this in my personal journal:

> The last few days here at the cabin have been unusually cold and windy for this time of year (near freezing at night). The leaves have been in full bloom for a couple of weeks but look very delicate still. I worry that the late cold will damage the fresh leaves and the force of the fierce winds tear off branches and even topple trees.
>
> Dear Lord, why do I grieve for the leaves and the trees when I know in my head that for them this extreme weather is a cleansing and a strengthening? Why do I grieve when adversity and tough challenges hit me in the face like a strong, cold wind, even though I know they will cleanse and strengthen me?
>
> I shall pick up the pieces of my broken trust, like fallen leaves and branches on the ground—and thank God for the cleansing and the strengthening of the winds and chills he sends my way or allows to come my way. And then I shall look further to the unmovable mountain

range on the horizon and think of God, who watches and waits to see my responses to adversity and assures me I'm in his providential care (May 11:2020).

Trusting God's trustworthiness is a humbling challenge, both for the insecure who need to see it proven right away and also for those self-reliant souls who are fiercely dependent on themselves to manage their own lives and fortunes. The former can be paralyzed by their helplessness, the latter by their arrogance. In a world of profound uncertainty and confusion, trusting God to fix things right away is desperation. And trusting nothing and no one outside our own wisdom and action is delusion.

When Jesus appears to his disciples following his resurrection, his first words are "Don't be afraid" or something similar. Don't be afraid: "Whoever believe in me will do the works that I do" (John 14:12). Don't be afraid: "The Holy Spirit will testify about me so that you can testify" (John 15:26-27). Don't be afraid: "I have conquered the world" (John 16:33c). These assurances have more to do with Christ's empowering presence than with our need for some immediate, miraculous evidence that he has come to fix things for us. They are about trusting his abiding presence without necessarily having the evidence or seeing it in action right away. We trust a person, not our own finite calculations of how exactly that person should act or what he specifically should do right now. And by the way, God is often full of surprises.

Sometimes God calls us to trust him by trusting ourselves. The decision to become a disciple of Jesus is not a decision to trust Jesus by distrusting ourselves. Our Lord does not hover over us, dictating our every step. He shows us the way and empowers us to walk in it. He shapes our soul and trusts us to discover and live out our holiness in his image. He revolutionizes our thinking and releases us to make decisions according to what the apostle Paul calls "the mind of Christ" (I Corinthians 2:16b). And when we mistake or misinterpret that mind—of which I have done my fair share—we will learn sooner or later how we missed the mark.

Jesus calls us to risk our lives for his sake and the gospel's (Mark 8:35). Following Jesus is a risk. He does not guarantee that when we follow him we will not get ourselves into trouble, as the early apostles did. How can we place ourselves in opposition to the present world order and then expect everyone to welcome us with open arms when they realize where we really stand and what we're really about? "In the world you have distress," says Jesus to his disciples. "But be encouraged. I have conquered the world" (John 16:33bc).

Unfortunately, some decide to follow Jesus in the hope he will keep them safe and their enemies at bay. Their Jesus is not the one we find in the Gospels. The Jesus of the Gospels lays down his life and calls his disciples to lay down *their* lives for his sake and the gospel's (Mark 8:34-37; Matthew 16:24-26; Luke 9:23-25). Why would we do this? We do it because we trust Jesus. Our lives are in his hands. When opposition threatens, like a raging storm and cold weather, we trust him. When we fear the damage will cause harm, we trust him to use it to cleanse and strengthen us. And we not only endure, we thrive!

Prayer

Humble Lord Jesus, thank you for showing me that my God can be trusted even when things are not going well and life is painful. Thank you for the countless ways you have been my Solid Rock in the storm. Please humble my pride, whether it's in the form of my insistence on immediate action on your part or my insistence that I am sufficient on my own. I ask in your name. Amen.

FRIDAY THE SECOND WEEK OF LENT
Risking Transparency

Scripture for Reflection: Psalm 32:2; 101:7;
Ephesians 4:11-16; 5:6-14: I John 1:5-10; I Peter 2:1-3, 21-22

Transparency is one of the incredibly disarming attributes of the humble. The humble may not be quick to speak, but when they do you sense they are not trying to impress or con you; they are telling you what they honestly see. In our success-driven world, however, "clever people" don't show their cards. Openness is seen as naïve, only our strengths and accomplishments are on display. We can and do bluff our way into acceptance and success, and the only people we trust with our fallibilities and failings are mostly professional counselors. In such a society of cultivated hiddenness and desperate self-promotion, transparency is the enemy. No wonder it scares us.

Adding to this fear of transparency is something the science of psychology has taught us about the relationship between our internal life and our external behavior. It has shown us that there are many layers of remembered experience and coping mechanisms we have internalized, much of it associated with pain avoidance, fear of failure, or survival. Some of this negative experience is repressed or lived out in unhealthy or inappropriate behaviors. How all of that internal stuff influences and determines our behaviors is hard to figure out, in myself and in others. How, then, is transparency about ourselves and others even possible for us?

The Bible connects human transparency with holiness, and hiddenness with sin. Adam and Eve's sin sends them into hiding and disconnects them from their open fellowship with God and each other. This loss of intimacy with God and with one another is a continuing thread for the remainder of the Old Testament. It expresses itself in our attempts to deceive God and one another, a deception that removes us from God's presence and drives wedges between us (Psalm 101; Proverbs 26:24-26). Fearing the threat of honesty and exposure, we "cling to deceit and refuse to return" to intimacy with God and one another (Jeremiah 8:4-6).

This is the situation into which Jesus comes—the perfectly transparent human who sees the truth in others, sees through all the barriers of pretense, sees us as we are, and wants to help us to be transparent. He wants us to see clearly and thank God for the good given us and in us. We all have some. He also wants us to ask God for the courage to see clearly the sin and the unhealthiness in us, confess it, and take steps to disempower and remove it. Our journey toward transparency begins with Christ who, says the apostle Peter, "left [us] an example so that [we] might follow in his footsteps. He committed no sin, nor did he speak in any ways meant to deceive" (I Peter 2:21b-22). At the beginning of that chapter, Peter admonishes his readers to get rid of "all deceit" if they intend to follow Jesus.

One of the most surprising statements made by Jesus is his greeting to Nathanael at their first meeting: "Here is a genuine Israelite in whom there is no deceit." How did Jesus know? Did he like the way Nathanael spoke his mind when, learning that this Jesus was from Nazareth, he said, "Can anything from Nazareth be good?" Or was it when he earlier and carefully observed Nathanael from a distance, while Nathanael was studying the Torah under a fig tree, as rabbis taught their disciples to do. Whatever the case might have been, Jesus liked the transparency and made him a disciple (John 1:45-49). Nathanael literally means "gift of God," and perhaps the name suggests the blessing of the transparent life.

What exactly is transparency? It is the willingness to see truth and reject deception when we see it, not with self-righteous judgments but with humility. It is the willingness to admit and confess our own limitations, our own prejudices and biases, and even our own sinful tendencies and shortcomings (I John 1:5-10), even as we humbly share our wisdom, our perspectives, or even prophetic words. We "grow in every way into Christ by speaking the truth with love" (Ephesians 4:11-16). This is also the only way spiritual and moral clarity will prevail. It is the only way we will be able to look at ourselves and each other with open minds and genuine hearts.

Transparency does not mean we are to be exhibitionists, exposing everything about ourselves to the world. It is not theater, it is worship. It is revealing the truth about ourselves and others in God's presence and humbly seeking a better truth. It is not spilling our guts to each other. It is looking into each other's hearts and seeing what God sees. Transparency is the end of deception. It is the gift God gives to the humble, the gift that can put an end to deception.

Prayer
Dear Jesus, thank you for showing us by your own life the beauty of transparency. Please bestow on me the grace to see myself clearly and to be honest and unpretentious before myself and others. And please clarify my view of others. Help me to see them as you see them so that I can love them as you love them. Please give me transparency, I pray in your name. Amen.

SATURDAY THE SECOND WEEK OF LENT
Living Without Excess

Scripture for Reflection: Matthew 6:25-34; Mark 10:23-25; II Corinthians 8:9; I Timothy 6:5-10, 17-19; James 5:1-6

Jesus knew what it was like to be without. He became a homeless man without material wealth, an itinerate rabbi who traveled light. He said of himself, "The Son of Man has nowhere to lay his head" (Matthew 8:20; Luke 9:58b). He does not, however, call his followers to be homeless; he calls them to be willing to live without excess, to discover the gift of unencumbered simplicity.

Consider excesses of personal wealth. Some people have gained wealth by exploiting or cheating others. Corrupt tax collector Zacchaeus, when he was summoned by Jesus, became convicted of his sin against vulnerable people, and he took immediate action to right the wrongs (Luke 19:8). Well, what about others who have gained their wealth fair and square? They certainly deserve to keep it and enjoy it (after taxes). Yes, as far as the law of the land says. But if we are talking about Jesus' law of love, which every Christian is called to follow, there must be spiritual integrity and depth to the answer. The wealthy young man who came to Jesus was a good person who diligently kept the commandments. There was no indication he had obtained his wealth by cheating. He seems to have been a good and well-respected person. Jesus, however, said he needed to do one thing more. It was the one thing he lacked, and not doing it put him in eternal danger. He needed to sell what he owned and give the money to the poor. According to Matthew's Gospel, Jesus said that this was what was required in order for the man to be "complete" and, according to all three Synoptic Gospels, what would ensure treasure in heaven and enable the young man to be Jesus' follower (Mark 10:17-21; Matthew 19:16-21; Luke 18:18-22). Obviously, Jesus knew that the man's wealth was too important and self-defining for him. It had become a competing god, or perhaps his real god underneath the layers of outward piety.

Every self-declared Christian of wealth needs to keep before her, and keep answering, these questions: Am I in danger of making my wealth my god? Am I using my wealth for the spiritual benefit of others (tithing) and to help meet the physical and social needs of the disadvantaged? Are my political decisions and my choice of candidates for office made primarily on the basis of what kind of government I believe will best help the people Jesus spent most of his time with, namely the less privileged?

Our discipleship has a lot to do with how we relate to material things and to money. If you think otherwise, just consider the fact that Jesus spoke many times more about money than about prayer. How we manage and spend our money is a discipleship question! The lust for wealth can afflict anyone. Even someone with meager resources can be possessed and driven by a lust for the very thing he doesn't have: money. The New Testament has a term for this soul-destroying longing: Mammon. Money that we devote our lives to accumulating and hording becomes our god Mammon.

Mammon is not the only god competing for a Christian's allegiance. Other seductive excesses draw us. Materialism, an addiction to a god called Things, can absorb and corrupt us. Philosopher Gabriel Marcel once observed that in our world we are taught how to take possession of things but not taught what we need more: how to let things go. "When there is too much," he said, "something is missing."

Another competing god is the lust for Fame. John the Baptist became a rather well-known and popular evangelist, but when he encountered someone who could easily have been seen as a competitor, he said to his disciples, "Look! The Lamb of God who takes away the sin of the world!" (John 1:29), and the next day two of his disciples left him and followed Jesus. Some people are consumed by their search for fame, even within the church, and it becomes a god, an addiction we cannot do without.

There are still other addictions that can so easily become gods: addictions to Power, Food, Alcohol, Drugs, to name a few. What is true of them all is that we feel or believe we cannot do without the "fix" they provide. We cannot say, "Enough." We convince ourselves there is never enough of what this false god gives us.

Jesus invites us to humble ourselves into an awareness of these gods that addict, disempower, and diminish us. He offers to liberate us from all such captivities. And he empowers and disciplines us to live without excess—without unnecessary Money, Things, Worldly Power, Fame, Food, Alcohol, Drugs, and whatever else may become our addiction, our god. Thanks be to the true and living God for his liberation!

Prayer
Dear God, I thank you for sending Jesus as our Way, our Truth, and our Life. I pray now for the liberation of those who live under the captivity of some addictive power over which they feel powerless. Please send alongside them those who will pray for them, encourage them, and travel with them to recovery. Please help me to pray for and help those I know who have been oppressed by the power of an addiction. And as I do so, help me to see and confess any excess that may have power over me. I pray this in the name of Jesus, our liberating Lord. Amen.

SUNDAY THE THIRD WEEK OF LENT
Jesus Healing Us

Scripture for Reflection: Isaiah 52:13-53:1-6; Matthew 8:17

Please read and meditate on the Scripture above before you start this meditation.

Israel had endured more than their fair share of suffering over the course of her history. Theirs was the suffering that at one time or another plagues every human being in this fallen world. Suffering is a part of life, even for those who are adept at pretending that everything is fine. We get sick, lose loved ones, make mistakes and suffer the consequences. There was another kind of suffering that Israel knew very well. It was the suffering that in one way or another followed their disobedience of God's covenant commands, or worse, followed their betrayal of his love. There was plenty of suffering to go around in Israel's story.

In Isaiah's startling passage, however, we hear of a very different kind of suffering. It's the suffering of someone called a "servant," a person who is "exalted and lifted very high" and yet now "appears disfigured, inhuman." He will "astonish many nations" and silence kings. Israel will see in this servant "what they haven't seen before." It will cause them to "ponder." This suffering servant will grow up in their midst, an expression of "the Lord's arm [strength or power]." And yet, because he has no hint of "splendor" or attractiveness, he will be "avoided by others," and people will hide their faces from him, despise him, and try to get him off their minds.

Then comes the real shocker. This suffering servant will carry their sickness and bear their sufferings, even though they "thought him afflicted, struck down by God and tormented." This suggests that the person Isaiah is describing will take upon himself their pain and sufferings, their unwellness. He does this because of their "rebellions and...crimes." He's a kind of scapegoat, carrying their sins well into the wilderness of their forgetfulness.

Who is this person? Isaiah doesn't identify him. You get the impression he doesn't know who he is talking about, only that this person will suffer terribly on behalf of God's chosen people.

The prophet doesn't stop there. He now plunges forward with the preposterous claim that the servant will bear their punishment and by doing so, make them whole. His wounding will bring their healing (v. 5). Not only does the servant suffer for them, his suffering actually heals them.

Centuries later, the early Christians came to see that this prophecy described their savior, Jesus. Matthew's Gospel describes Jesus' healing ministry as the fulfillment of this prophecy (Mathew 8:17). The apostle Peter endorses the same understanding (I Peter 2:22-24). Jesus endured more suffering than we can imagine. And what the Gospels are telling us is that he did it because we were sick and needed healing.

Sickness is one very helpful way to understand our sin and its consequences. It is when something in our lives isn't healthy or working as it should. Soul sickness is when our spiritual life is immobilized or misdirected. Emotional sickness is when our emotional life is undermining our mental health. Relational sickness is when our relationships with others are damaging or damaged. Physical sickness is when some part of our body is in pain or under threat. Body-of-Christ sickness is when a church is not living her calling to love God, each other, and the world. Missional sickness is when the church's outreach to others is either ineffective or non-existent. We shall be looking at each of these sicknesses and their healing over the course of this week.

For today, let's focus on Jesus as a healer. The Gospel records show him to be a prodigious healer. He heals persons who are physically sick or handicapped, emotionally disturbed, relationally isolated, or socially discriminated against. The thing that makes his healings unique is that not only are they motivated by his compassion toward all who suffer (Matthew 14:14), but there often seems to be an accompanying spiritual healing, whether explicitly revealed (Matthew 9:2) or implied by what follows (Mark 5:1-20). The four men who bring their crippled friend to Jesus for healing are surprised when the physical healing takes place after Jesus tells the man that his sins are forgiven (Matthew 9:1-8). There is, it seems, some kind of deep relationship between spiritual sickness—for example, sins that need to be forgiven— and the need for other kinds of healing.

The church is the Body of Christ in which the illness of one part of the Body affects the whole Body (I Corinthians 12:26). In a similar way each of us is comprised of many dimensions and parts, each having an effect on the others. Jesus' healing ministry demonstrated that he could identify the illness and apply the cure. He also knew the danger of his healing power: that people would flock to him for easy healing and would adore him for "fixing" them.

Jesus is not a fixer or a fix. He doesn't fix us, he frees us. He releases and empowers us to become who God created us to be. He is interested in far more than our illnesses, whatever they are. He is interested in the kind of health that makes us holy persons—even if we don't get physically well, even if we still have to grapple with some painful memories, even if we can't "fix" all the damaged relationships in our lives. Jesus came to us to penetrate our suffering by pouring out his life into them and taking away their power over us.

Whatever sicknesses may threaten us, Jesus invites us to bring them to him for healing. As we see in the healing miracles of Jesus, what he asks of us is faith. "Your faith has made you well," we hear him say again and again. It is not magic he performs; it is healing. Magic is always fake; healing always life-changing.

Prayer
Healing Lord, I bring to you whatever threatens my well-being as your child. (You may want to name that threat here: _____ _____.) I ask for your healing touch, for a better understanding of my illness, and for the faith to receive your healing and to live in it. I ask this in the name of Jesus, who gave his life so that we all can be well. Amen.

MONDAY THE THIRD WEEK OF LENT
Soul Healing

Scripture for Reflection: Luke 5:27-32; II Corinthians 3:18

What exactly is a *soul*? The word is a common English translation of a New Testament Greek word that means *our very being*. Our soul is the very essence of who we are. It is not some piece or part of us. It *is* us. The Bible teaches that we are embodied souls with hearts (the source of our motivation and will) and minds (our capacity to remember and think). This helps us understand what Jesus meant when he said the first commandment is that we are to "love the Lord your God with all your heart, and with all your being [soul], and with all your mind" (Matthew 22:37; also Mark and Luke).

The most essential healing we need is soul healing, the healing of our very being. As the Genesis account of the fall of humankind makes clear and the rest of Scripture confirms, our most basic problem is that our very being is sick. Our souls, shaped in the image of God, were created to reflect him, commune with him, love and adore him, live in ways that bring him pleasure, and choose to obey him. *Choose*, not comply, to obey him: God's gift of freedom. We are given the option, if you like, to go another way, to have *our* way. And when we choose to do so, our souls fall ill. Designed to reflect and imitate God (Ephesians 5:1), we instead grasp at straws, which at first seem so attractive and appealing to our egos, until in a moment of sober truth, we realize we have only become straw men and women. We are trying to be who we are not.

We were made to worship God, and when we worship anything else—ourselves, our careers, our pious behavior, our acquisitions, our successes, our indulgences, our addictions, or any number of other idols—we are soul sick. We are not being who we are, we are living a lie, we are not whole. We were made to love God and others—even our enemies—and when our love for ourselves supersedes these loves, we are suffocating our souls.

The God who created this universe through Christ his Son (Colossians 1:15-18) sent his Son to incarnate himself in the physical, now fallen, creation. He did it through the person of Jesus. Jesus' mission was and is to open the door to wholeness. He did it by teaching us to live in the healthy environment of the kingdom of God, and he made it possible by the healing effect of his life, suffering, and crucifixion, and by his resurrection from death.

The healing of the soul cannot be completed in one fell swoop. As we grow in grace, the healing continues. Step by step over a lifetime, our calling is to be changed into the image of Christ, from one degree to the next, through the Spirit (II Corinthians 3:18). This is what we signed up for when we brought our broken souls to Christ. Conversion is the initial work of healing grace. Living our lives from then on is the continued work of grace in our lives, moving us toward the image of Christ and the ongoing healing of our brokenness.

When Jesus accepted the tax collector Levi's invitation to a banquet attended largely if not entirely by known sinners, the religious critics were quick to condemn his actions as incomprehensible for a true spiritual leader. Jesus' answer carried two meanings. First the obvious one: These sinners are sick and need the presence and healing of a physician. Second, the hidden meaning (but no less real): If only you righteous people knew your own need for healing of the brokenness your pious exteriors mask, I would be able to change your hearts and lives. But I can't because you keep hiding behind your surface piety, and that makes you incapable of responding to my call (Luke 5:27-32).

As a young convert to Christ, I thought my Christian life would fall into place nicely. I figured Christ would have my back and see me through. After all, I was active in church and did my devotions. I tried to be good, even if it frequently amounted to little more than pretense. Over time, I began to realize that conversion was not magic, a sudden, automatic fix. It was the promise of a life of transformation. It was a spiritual journey with a reliable Guide, and the journey was internal because the Guide was the Guardian and Physician of my soul. The Guide was Christ, and his agenda for me was the healing of my brokenness (sin) when I was ready and desirous enough for yet another step-in transformation.

Our soul's healing is a lifelong journey with our Healer. Perhaps you can join me in this prayer for that journey for yourself.

Prayer
Dear Christ, please reveal to me the next step in my soul's journey toward your likeness. (The reader may want to identify that step here: _____.)
And I ask for your grace to enable me to take that step and become a person closer to that likeness. I ask this in your name, the Physician of my soul. Amen.

TUESDAY THE THIRD WEEK OF LENT
Emotional Healing

Scripture for Reflection: Luke 15:11-24; 7:36-50;
Matthew 8:18-27; John 20:19-23

Our emotions are God's gift. They telegraph the feeling-effect of what we are experiencing. Good feelings affirm the pleasure of what we are experiencing; bad feelings the unpleasantness or threat; mixed feelings the uncertainty or suspicion. Our emotions help us make our judgments and form our responses.

How well we use our emotions to shape good decisions depends upon the level of our emotional stability. An insecure person might exaggerate a threat and be immobilized by it. A detached person might be unable to see it or deal with it. There are back stories to our emotions. Painful past experiences may adversely influence how well we are able to celebrate good experiences and recognize real threats. All this to say that our emotions are complex. Therapists spend a lot of time trying to help disturbed people sort out their emotions and discover some of the root causes of their emotional suffering.

How does the healing ministry of Jesus address the health of our emotional life? Sometimes Jesus encountered people who clearly needed emotional healing. In that day, a person's emotional life was not talked about as much as it has been since the advent of psychology and psychiatry. Now our emotional reactions are studied and scientifically classified, and treatments abound for profusions of unhealthy emotional reactions. Even with all the therapeutic tools at our disposal today, I'm not convinced the percentage of the population who are emotionally well has increased. It has probably decreased due to instability in families, faith communities, relationships, neighborhoods, and many other factors.

Jesus did not speak the language of psychology, but he sensed the deep pain some were feeling. In this brief meditation, we will focus on two: guilt feelings and fear.

Jesus was sensitive to the pain inflicted by guilt. In one parable, he tells of a son who squanders his inheritance, now coming home heavy with guilt about taking advantage of his father's love. On another occasion, a woman looked down upon for being disreputable kneels before Jesus. Without a word, she wipes Jesus' dust-stained feet with the tearful flow of her love, and then stands and applies the oil of her worship over his head.

Guilt is a powerful emotion, a prison the release from which is a fresh start. The prodigal son returns home hoping for the least: servitude, where before his sin he had sonship. Instead, he is embraced in the grace of his father's loving arms and given a banquet worthy of a son. On another occasion, Jesus attends a banquet hosted by a pharisee, where a sinful woman slips in unnoticed. The disreputable woman kneels before Jesus knowing she deserves no more than expulsion from the banquet and from association with "good people." The host—and probably every other dinner guest—is shocked that Jesus allows such "intimate" contact from a well-known sinner. Our Lord, however, knowing what everyone is thinking, shocks everyone by honoring the woman for doing what the host was supposed to have seen to. And then, using a simple analogy of the greater the debt the more the love toward the forgiver, he receives her love and affirms her faith.

If guilt is an emotional disabler, grace is the enabler. The greater the awareness of our guilt (as with the prodigal son and the sinful woman), the greater our love toward the forgiver. Perhaps the problem of some Christians today is their inability to confess the hidden sins, owning only the trivial sins on the surface. The elder son in the parable and the pharisee at the banquet would have done well to look deeper into their own hearts to see and then confess the more subtle but all the more powerful sins behind their self-righteousness. Guilt can suppress the inner voice of honesty and hide behind "proper behavior."

Another emotion that plagues us is fear. Fear is a helpful emotion when real danger is near. But fear can also immobilize us when it emerges from painful or harmful experiences in the past and is triggered by something in the present that suggests a possible recurrence of the repressed experience.

Jesus certainly understood fear. His own disciples were overcome with fear more than once when caught in storms on the lake. Their fear was calmed only by the presence of Jesus, once when he was awakened from sleep and another time when he came to them walking on water. After Jesus' death, they were again seized by fear and cowered in hiding. They hope they wouldn't be found by those who might be set on doing away with them, as well. Again, it is the sudden awareness of Jesus' palpable presence that calms their fears.

Jesus is the healer of our fears. He doesn't remove them, he faces them. He situates himself with them and says to us, "What you fear has no power over me and who you are because of me." Jesus is the healer of our guilt. He situates himself with sinners like us and says, "This is not who you are, not who you were created to be. Don't be like the elder brother in the parable or the Pharisee at the banquet; don't hide your sin beneath righteous pretense. Let me be your Lord and Healer." Guilt and fear are disabling emotions. There are other emotions that can sometimes disable us. Jesus is our Healer in every case, by whatever good friend, counselor, pastor, or church represents him.

Prayer
Dear healing Christ, my emotions may sometimes hurt me or even cripple me. I thank you for those feelings that help and strengthen me, and I surrender to you for your healing of those feelings that disable me. I ask this and claim healing in your name. Amen.

WEDNESDAY THE THIRD WEEK OF LENT
Relational Healing

Scripture for Reflection: Matthew 10:34-36; Luke 16:19-31; 10:25-37

Almost immediately following the account of the Fall, Scripture leads us through an extended parade of broken human relationships. Sin against God brings sin against other people. We break our relationship with God, and our relationships with one another suffer. And when our relationships with others are broken, our relationship with God is affected. Love of God and love of one another are of a piece. To claim one but not the other is to deceive ourselves (I John 4:20).

Is it possible to live life without some experiences of relationship breakups? Probably not. When break-ups do happen, the issue for we who are followers of Jesus is what our attitude toward the other person becomes. Do we see him or her as a child of God, still deserving of our love, even if that person has betrayed us? Is Jesus asking the impossible of us—love your enemies and those who despitefully use you?

The answer is yes, but it is unmistakably a tough yes. Loving someone who is opposed to our lifestyle, ethics, or beliefs is one thing. Loving someone who has done us ill is another. Love can cross boundaries of strong differences, but it must blindly crash through the emotional barriers of deep hurt, carried by an indiscriminate Christ-like love that transcends even abuse. To forgive the one who has hurt us deeply is the gift of the all-forgiving, crucified Jesus. It is the most powerful of relational healing among humans. It is the miracle of God.

Some hurt—and sometimes a lot of hurt—takes place within

our families. Every family has its squabbles, at least occasionally. Any family that doesn't is probably following a code of silence about their anger, burying it deep within their individual psyches—until it reveals itself in unhealthy, unhelpful ways. No human has understood what was in the heart of a person as Jesus did. He saw through the external behavior and drew out what was really there, as with the woman who washed Jesus' feet with her tears, using her own hair. He called out in her what she felt she had no right to claim: her saving faith and her deep love (Luke 7:36-50). So with the man who pleaded with Jesus to make his brother give him the justice he deserved—"justice" being his part of the family inheritance. Jesus looked into the man's heart and saw not a sincere desire for justice but a dangerous greed (Luke 12:13-15). According to Jesus, family divisions are best dealt when the pretenses are put aside and the real motives are openly confessed.

Strange as it may seem, family relationships can also be seriously damaged when the family sees itself as something approaching the stature of God. Yes, a family can become its own idol, an object of worship. In the words of Jesus, those who love their parents or children more than they love him are not worthy of him (Matthew 10:37). Families lacking in love are indeed sick families; families totally absorbed in worshipful love for each other are also sick families. If our families are the most important thing in our lives, they diminish us by subordinating our love for God and stunting our compassion for others. A family can be broken by its excessive attentiveness to itself.

Another area of relational healing finds Jesus once again leading the way. As a Jewish rabbi, he refocused his followers on the calling of the Hebrews to be a blessing to the nations. We cannot actually bless without including. To bless someone is to include them as part of your life and to include yourself in theirs. Blessing is the doorway to inclusion. As a Jew called first to the Jews, Jesus, step by step, began to widen the boundaries of his mission beyond Judaism. His itinerate mission included not only Judah, but also and primarily Galilee (not considered by the Judeans as authentically Jewish as Judah), and then to Samaria, an area intentionally avoided by Jewish travelers, as if it were contaminated by paganism. The Gospel records also mention foreigners (some of them undoubtedly not Jewish) traveling some distance to hear him or be healed by him—all of them welcomed!

Jesus launched—and the apostle Paul vigorously pursued—a barrier-breaking mission of inclusiveness. No border was too far to cross, no social or ethnic group too "different" to exclude.

In my own country at this time, events have exposed persistent racial and ethnic divides that call for healing. Followers of Jesus in particular are called to respond by becoming agents of reconciliation. (We shall return to this important calling on Saturday of this week.) For now, begin to pray for a Christ-given understanding of how you can contribute to Christ-given solutions to damaged relationships you may have in your own life and those in your community, city, and nation.

Prayer

Lord God, thank you for sending Jesus to bring healing not only to our souls but also to our relationships. Holy Spirit of Jesus, I ask you for insight into those relationships in my life where healing is needed, and I ask your guidance in how to release and trust your healing love in those relationships. I also pray for the healing of brokenness between ethnic and racial groups, and I ask for guidance in the role you want me to play in that healing mission. I ask these things in the name of our Wonderful Healer, Jesus the Christ. Amen.

THURSDAY THE THIRD WEEK OF LENT
Physical Healing

Scripture for Reflection: Luke 4:18; Matthew 8:14-17

Jesus was intensely interested in the physical health of people. He saw bodily disease and impairment as a condition to heal, not simply something about which to console the sufferer. When he found Peter's mother-in-law sick at home with a fever, he touched her, and the fever left. She went on to continue her domestic duties as hostess, as if her healing was an event in the natural flow of the day. Then "people brought to Jesus many who were demon-possessed…[and] sick." All were healed as the "natural flow" of the day continued. I describe these healing events as a part of the "natural flow" of Jesus' day, not to diminish the healings but to underline that they were not some magic power displays to impress the gullible; they were natural outcomes of who Jesus was and is for those who believe in him. He is not just a healer, he is healing itself!

Most of the physical healing in Jesus' ministry seems to have been directed toward persistent diseases and impairments that had long victimized the sufferers. The condition for healing was simply faith in the Healer, Jesus. It would seem that the healing was a painless process for the recipients. Think again. As wonderful as the restoration of the diseased or broken body was, the life change that the person—and his family!— had to make would have been major, even painful. A contemporary example that comes to mind is that of a long-time alcoholic who comes to sobriety, but finds it extremely difficult to find his place in a family that has for some time reconfigured its dynamics around the person's active addiction, maybe has even had to no longer rely on, or even trust, the person. The family healing may be a long, painful process. Another example is a physically impaired person who must now become self-reliant after living his whole life relying on others. Surgery is another example: the healing process following surgery may be long and painful. One way or another, the process of real healing is not easy.

At this point, we would do well to raise a question about our participation in our own healing. It seems to me that it makes sense to ask God to heal our bodies only if we are being good stewards of our bodies. Is it even respectful of God to ask him to fix something about our health or physical condition if and as we continue to pursue behaviors that abuse or exploit our bodies? For example, if we are workaholics who push (exploit) our bodies unmercifully—I've personally been there—or if we deal with stress by overeating, it's hardly fair of us to ask God to heal the sicknesses caused by our behavior while we continue the behavior that brought on the sickness! If it's real healing we want, we must be participants with God in the process.

The promise of healing has become an economic enterprise that deceives people with exaggerated and often totally false claims of painless healing power. Because of clever advertisements we may even begin to imagine we have the dreaded condition and therefore buy the miracle product. We are a society of presumed illnesses and probable pains, for all of which there is always a painless cure.

All real healing is painful. There are people who have the gift of healing (I Corinthians 12:9). Their very presence can be a reminder of the healing Christ, their touch a balm. What distinguishes them is that they themselves do not do the healing; they are conduits of the healing Christ. What we must be cautious about are self-proclaimed "faith healers" who build personal empires with their healing shows, promote emotionally charged mass gatherings, and render a hypnotic effect on people desperately wanting healing, all the while lacking the humility of the real healer.

Someone has said that we're making too much of faith healing and not enough of healing faith. Faith healing promises an instantaneous fix, healing faith promises a process of genuine healing. One does little for the soul, the other purifies and strengthens it. When faith healing "fails" by not accomplishing the specific healing the healer demands that God perform, and the person is left with nothing but a failure. When healing faith does not accomplish the complete physical healing, the person is left with a deepened faith and the assurance that God is with him and will manifest his healing in ways that give real joy and a witness, the credibility of which will turn heads, and hearts.

Health is holistic. It involves more than our physical body. It involves our soul, our emotional lives, our relationships with people. Our faith is at work in all these dimensions, bringing new healing, new life, new joy. This is why a very physically fit person can be miserable because he is deeply sick in his soul, his emotions, and his relational life. And this is why a person dying of cancer can convey a true health in spite of the cancer, because her soul rejoices in the Lord, her love for others is undeniable, and no person or circumstance can rob her of her joy.

Prayer
Dear Christ, who in Jesus took the form of our human bodies, help me to trust the natural flow of your healing. I bring my own body to you to use for your glory by my stewardship of it, with whatever imperfections or infirmities it may have. Through Christ, my Lord and Healer, I pray, Amen.

FRIDAY THE THIRD WEEK OF LENT
Church Healing

Scripture for Reflection: Ephesians 2:11-22;
I Corinthians 1:10-13; 3:1-9, 21-22

When Steven Eliot returned from his last term of military service in the Middle East War, he needed healing. He reported that the healing only began when he was able to say, "I am not well," and began reaching out to others ("War Story," interview on MSNBC, 4/4/19). God never intended for us to suffer alone. He gave us communities for healing. He gave us his church, a place of healing for those who can confess to Christian brothers and sisters their need for healing. The church is called to be a community where the need for healing is not an embarrassment but a requirement for membership. So long as members know that, they can be agents of healing for each other and for others who need healing.

The old hymn, "What a friend we have in Jesus," has these lines: "O what needless pain we bear,/ All because we do not carry/ Everything to God in prayer." These lines omit that God's plan is also for the church to share burdens through the healing presence and support of brothers and sisters in Christ. The only people mentioned in the hymn are "friends [who] despise [and] forsake." If we see our need of healing as a matter between us and God, never shared with others, we reject Christ's gift, the church.

The church is called to be a community of healing. There are some congregations that are themselves unhealthy. The communal sickness can take different forms. Perhaps the most dangerous is when the congregation has lost its purpose and its character. Some congregations are like clubs that come together to enjoy one another's company and align themselves with a creed that gives them comfort and assurance without demanding radical change through Christ and compassionate outreach in his name. Their sickness is all the more insidious for the veneer of a smooth operation that hides the spiritual death underneath. Healing for such a congregation can take place only with the rediscovery of what the church is really called to be and do. It would amount to a spiritual revolution, whether sudden or gradual, and the possible loss of some members who are not open to their club becoming a New Testament church.

Some congregations are unhealthy because they are divided into competitive groups. The division may be family based, leadership based, or both. A congregation may be sick because two warring family groups compete for congregational control, and many in the congregation get caught up in the competition for turf and power. Similarly, a congregation may be divided because group members develop a loyalty to the leadership of a particular person. All such competitive groups undermine the health and effectiveness of the whole congregation. The congregation exhausts itself with infighting.

The apostle Paul had to face the leader-based, divisive groups in the Corinthian congregation. One group aligned with Apollos, another with Cephas (Peter), another with Paul, and—believe it or not—another with Christ. Four competing groups with their own leader, Christ being only one of those leaders. Paul uses such labels as unspiritual, babylike, jealousy-driven, in-fighting, people-without-the-Spirit to describe the congregation. He affirms these leaders at a crucial time in the congregation's development. They are not competing, however, they are "workers together," all building on the one foundation, Jesus Christ. No group in the congregation is more important than the other. Everything belongs to them all. They all belong to Christ, and Christ to God. A congregation with divided loyalties is a broken body.

In his Ephesian Letter, Paul addresses the first big leap of Christianity from a Jewish to a Gentile church. We can read about this transfer from Jewish-exclusive to Gentile-inclusive in Acts and Galatians. It was a painful transition made possible and irresistible through the reconciling death of Jesus on the cross: two ethnicities comprising one body of Christ. It was the beginning of the true church, which even to this day often struggles to be who she really is: a community loyal to the radical inclusiveness of Jesus, a body of believers with arms open to the whole world with a message, backed up by action, that says, "You are welcome here. Our family has a place for you, whatever your ethnicity or race."

As you pray the following prayer, apply it to your own congregation if any area of its life and witness needs healing.

Prayer
Dear Lord, Healer of our wounds, I ask that you reveal to me the healing I need to pray for in my congregation: the healing we need in order to be your holy, inclusive Body, a credible expression of God's love for the whole world, and a compelling witness to others. Dear Lord, I want to be a uniter, not a divider. If there is any way I am a barrier to the healing of my church, please reveal it to me so that I can confess it and by your grace overcome or remove it. I pray this in the name of the One who is over all, in all, and for all. Amen.

SATURDAY THE THIRD WEEK OF LENT
Inclusive Healing

Scripture for Reflection: Luke 11:37-41;
II Corinthians 5:13-21

In his poem "Mending Wall," Robert Frost wonders why the wall between his and his neighbor's property must always be kept in repair. The neighbor's rationale is simply: "Good fences make good neighbors." Frost wonders what they were "walling in or walling out." There were no roaming cows on either side, and their respective trees would not think of trespassing. The poet is trying to understand why we love our walls, and why there's something in him that definitely doesn't love a wall.

Think about all the walls we build: around homes to separate ourselves from neighbors or at borders to keep out immigrants. Such walls are testimony to a human race that doesn't trust a neighbor or tolerate differences. They are the wraparounds of our fears, the protections of our hatreds, the testimony to our sinful dividedness. They are the symbols of countless unseen walls, more powerful than they seem precisely because they are more difficult to identify, and easier to deny. "I'm no racist," some may insist, while they quietly do their best to protect their neighborhood from encroachment. Inclusion can be practiced in ways that are very awkward, difficult, or impossible for the outsider to negotiate. And the politics, economics, and educational systems of a city may well serve to strengthen the walls.

I vividly remember the summer of 1963. Keitha and I were part of a coffee house ministry in Chicago. The coffee house was situated where five streets converged. The streets created a pie effect. Each of four of the slices of the pie was comprised of a distinct ethnic and racial community: Black, Hungarian Gypsy, Appalachian White, and Puerto Rican. We had a policy of inclusion: teenagers from any of those ethnic groups were welcome on any night. But policy is one thing, implementation another. As it turned out, on any given night, only one of those groups was present. Each racial/ethnic group had its night. The groups were not going to mix. These teens had learned the rules of exclusionary behavior.

Such a state of affairs is understandable in light of the dividing walls of separation created by our fallenness. In the previous meditation, however, we saw how in Christ, those who were separated have been brought near to God and to his people by the cross (Ephesians 2:13). God really was in Christ reconciling the world to himself, changing us from enemies into friends and giving us the ministry of making others his friends (II Corinthians 5:18). And as we have seen, being a true friend of God means being friends with our fellow human beings. Does this ministry of inclusion extend only to people who look and act like us? If God's mission is "to bring all things together in Christ" (Ephesians 1:10), could that mission possibly exclude any person or group, no matter the economic condition, the race, or ethnicity? The answer is clear—but the willingness of many Christians is murky. As we have seen, the Scriptures affirm that God is the creator of all humanity, Christ's mission crosses all human barriers, and the church is called to complete that inclusive mission. This missional calling goes back as far as Abraham pleading with God on behalf of pagan Sodom (Genesis 18:16-33), immigrant Ruth overwhelmed and surprised that the Jew Boaz has treated her so graciously and inclusively (Ruth 2:10-13), and the Jewish law itself, which commanded Jews to treat immigrants and strangers "as if they were one of your citizens"—even "to love them as yourself" (Leviticus 19:34). Christians see Jesus as one who opens the way to union with God and with all his creation. A human race divided by exclusions is not God's gift; a human race united in love and enjoying the diversity is.

Given the polarized world we live in, the unifying gift of God in Christ seems to be an impossibly naïve dream. So how do we take seriously the mission of Christ in the fullness of time to bring all things together in him (Ephesians 1:10)? Is it truly "Christian" for us to claim there's really nothing we can do, only Christ is up to the task? "When he comes again, he'll fix everything." That is the kind of cop-out that has gotten us into the fix we're in. It seems to me there are two ways forward. The first is to ask the Holy Spirit to release us from our ethnic and racial narrowness, to empower us to see beyond our own cultural prejudices, and to motivate us to reach out in some authentic way to a person or persons of a different color or ethnicity to build relationships.

The second way forward is also essential. For us to expect the excluded to be content to wait for Christians and others to finally get enlightened to act in accord with the inclusive gospel is, well, demeaning in and of itself. Without political action of some kind, social justice will not be done. Even if a follower of Jesus is not comfortable with being personally involved in social action, she can vote in a way that is primarily supportive of the socially excluded and pray for those who take risks on their behalf.

Our society is in need of healing. Do we trust our Divine Healer enough to give us an inclusive heart and to empower us to act in the best way we can to bring healing where there is brokenness?

Prayer

As you pray, ask the Lord to reveal to you a specific way you can initiate a relationship of reconciliation with someone of another race or ethnicity, or, decide and implement some specific step(s) to support justice for the excluded.

SUNDAY THE FOURTH WEEK OF LENT
Jesus Re-Creating Us

Scripture for Reflection: Colossians 1:15-20; 3:8-11

As followers of Jesus, we are re-creations. To say that is to say that we had an earlier first creation. It is also to say that there is a connection between our first and our new creation. The "re" in re-creation means that our second creation is a return to who we were intended to be in the first place. It's as if a painter's masterpiece has become seriously damaged, and he paints another version of the same work of art. Perhaps the new work is even better because the painter has himself now grappled with the deeper meaning and purpose of the painting. He has, if you like, put all of himself into this new painting.

The artist in this analogy is, of course, Christ—Christ, Son of God, the Word of God, the Artist of all creation. As the Nicene Creed says, "Without him [Christ] was not anything made that was made…" Creation, however, does not stop with that first creative act of God. If we believed it did, we would be Deists, who tend to think that after initial creation, God kept his distance and left us to it. Christians believe, and Scriptures testify, that God is deeply involved in this world. The divine Christ continues to be with and in everything—even very bad people, or they couldn't exist! Or we couldn't love them as Jesus commands us to do! Christ is in them, waiting to be born so that they can become who they were created to be.

Christ is both our Creator and our Re-Creator. In the first creation, he made all the wonderful stuff and all the life that throbbed throughout this vast universe. He made everything and everyone, and he still does. And without him nothing can continue to exist. Christ is, indeed, "all things and in all people" (Colossians 3:11), and "all things are held together in him" (1:17). Christ never left us; he's there or we wouldn't exist.

So why is the world in the mess it's in? The short answer is "choices." God decided to give humans the capacity to choose who or what to worship and to love. Bad choices were made and continue to be made, so much so that we forgot who we were and why we were. We were lost from God and from ourselves. A new creation, a re-creation was needed. This time Christ the Creator became one of us to re-create us, not from the outside but from the inside. He came in the form of a human, as a man named Jesus—perfectly God, perfectly human. He came to be with us to show us and teach us who we were meant to be from the beginning of creation. He came to show us life by his living and to give us life through the life-releasing healing of his crucifixion. Like that painter who put all of himself into the re-creation of his painting, Christ the divine Painter put all of himself and all of his artistry into the flesh and blood of Jesus of Nazareth to show us what it means to be fully human.

Christian writer Andy Raine suggests that we Christians have focused so much on original sin that we have forgotten original innocence (Celtic Daily Prayer, II, p. 1518). It's as if that innocence is now so far from reality that it is best left alone, and Christians can only hope they do not sin so much as to lose their credibility as believable followers of Jesus or lose heaven. It's true that the original innocence in the Garden has long gone. Bad choices were made, and we sinned. But Christ came in the flesh and blood of Jesus to show us how to be fully human (holy) again. He came as our Rabbi to teach us the Way. He said if we lived by his teaching we'd be as stable as a house built on solid rock, and if we didn't, we'd be like a house built on sand (Luke 6:46-49). He suffered for us and died for us so that we could die to our false selves and find in him our true selves that we call souls (Galatians 2:20). He was resurrected so that his Spirit could abide with us and even in us, guide us, and enable us (John 16:12-16; Galatians 5:16-26). Jesus is the masterpiece that holds our gaze and defines our lives as Christians.

The Lenten Season invites us to behold the masterpiece and find ourselves in it. It may take us a while to see what we need to see. We may at first fail to see our worthiness, but over time, Jesus will catch us with eyes that tell us that the value of our lives is beyond calculation. We may at first want him to see our spiritual accomplishments, but he draws us to himself to love who we are—far, far more than what we've done. Or we may want to complain to him about the raw deal life has dealt us, but he tells us he has never left or forsaken us; he has suffered with us, cried with us, and actually given us the strength to endure.

We probably won't see such things at first. Seeing what the masterpiece has to tell us usually takes time. A real masterpiece has more to reveal to us than we see at first. The revelation may come as a gift of quiet meditation. It may come after searching and engaging the Scriptures. It may come from the depths of a musical composition that penetrates your heart like an arrow. It may come from what you observe in another person or receive from that person.

Marlene Chase tells a story about Anthony, the father of the monastic movement in the early Christian church. Three monks used to visit Anthony every year. Two of the monks would discuss their thoughts and the salvation of their souls. The third monk had nothing to say and no questions to ask. After a few years, Anthony said to him, "You often come to see me, but you never ask me anything." The monk replied, "It is enough to see you, Father" (The War Cry, 11/25/00).

Jesus Christ offers to take the good and bad of our lives and make a masterpiece of it. Most great masterpieces reflect a depth of life; they are rarely just "pretty." They reveal something of our brokenness or how healing and hope have come out of that brokenness. It's the same with our lives. Our miraculous re-creation in Christ is that kind of masterpiece. The more the brokenness, the greater the miracle.

When I visit the Sunday morning worship service at an Adult Rehabilitation Center (the name of a residential addiction recovery ministry operated by The Salvation Army), I am always struck by the testimonies of the people in recovery. Their words come out of deep places of brokenness. They know where they have been, and some of them know they are not yet where they need to be in their recovery. The honesty is palpable, the confession genuine. Sometimes it makes me think about myself and forces me to confess that the masterpiece Christ wants to make of my life is far from finished.

It's easy to pretend, and I've done my fair share. So, when I'm honest about this or that sin, or about my neglect, or about my self-righteousness, I go to Christ, the divine Painter, and ask him to help me with the canvas of my life. And with the purifying paint of his forgiveness and grace, he touches something on the canvas and gives me a further glimpse of who and what I am because of my re-creation in him. Then he says to me, "You are free and empowered to be that person. I will help you."

Perhaps you would like to join me in praying the following prayer:

Prayer
Lord, I bring to you my self-constructed image of myself, and I confess that there are aspects of it that block who you are trying to make of me. Please reveal to me, by whatever means you choose, the next step in my re-creation, and by your grace empower me to take that step regardless of the cost or the pain or the embarrassment. I pray this in your name. Amen.

MONDAY THE FOURTH WEEK OF LENT
Jesus Re-Creating Our Heart

Scripture for Reflection: Matthew 5:8;
Ephesians 4:17-24; Revelation 2:1-4

The English word "heart" is a moving target. It can mean the source of very unreliable emotions that can be up one moment and down the next, depending on external circumstances, internal conflicts, or causes we can't even identify. The word may express a resolve, as in "He really has a heart for his work." Or it may describe the depth of someone's love for another person: "I love her with all my heart."

The New Testament uses the word "heart" (*kardia* in New Testament Greek) in different ways. Each of them invites us to consider an aspect of our lives that may be ready for Christ's re-creative ministry. As we consider some of them, you may discover one or two that speak to your own spiritual desire or need at this time in your journey with Jesus.

Let's begin with uses of the word "heart" to describe our capacity to see God, or blind ourselves to him. The psalmist David says, "Fools say in their hearts, 'There is no God'" (Psalm 14:1a). Jesus says that those with pure hearts are happy because they will see God (Matthew 5:8). Of course, we cannot now actually see God…or can we? Did he not appear in the flesh and blood of Jesus of Nazareth, and do not the Gospels continually draw us to this man, this man who is not only fully a human but also fully God? The pure of heart, said Jesus, have been given eyes to see God, and the band of Jesus' disciples, as they became more and more acquainted with Jesus, finally came to the recognition that when they were looking at Jesus, they were looking into the face of God. Perhaps you are at a place in your spiritual journey where you need to let yourself spend time seeing God in the face and life of Jesus. It could lead to a newer creation in your life.

Sometimes the heart itself is an impediment. The psalmist speaks of God's people actually hardening their hearts by not trusting him and not listening to him for the forty wilderness years the Hebrews spent after Moses led them out of Egypt. Their hearts became so twisted and distorted that God turned away from them (Psalm 95:8-11). Fast forward to the two sorrowful travelers on the road to Emmaus a few days after Jesus' crucifixion. As they tried to make sense of the death of their Lord, they were joined by another traveler whom they at first did not recognize. The traveler asked them what they were discussing. Surprised that the stranger didn't seem to know about the terrible tragedy, they began briefly to describe the horrible events of the past few days. Their story concluded with puzzlement: Who took Jesus' body from the tomb? Jesus responded to them by saying their hearts were slow, and for the rest of their time together, he spoke of his suffering and death as fulfillment of prophecy. Over the supper table, as they looked into the face of a resurrected Jesus breaking bread, they now saw God. If you have yourself experienced a slowness of heart, perhaps you need to let yourself have some meals with Jesus, maybe with another fellow traveler or two.

Jesus says our heart is defined by what we treasure (Luke 12:34). If we treasure God's will, our heart throbs with life; if we treasure our own worthless idols, our heart is as dead as a stone (Ezekiel 36:26-27). You may want to take a hard look at your treasury—who or what you are most investing your life in. You may want to make more space in your day for what Christ tells you has greater worth. By doing so you will place your heart in a better treasury, and you will free your life for more of Christ's re-creation of your heart.

God knows our heart, our true self. He made it so that we would find our way to him. He made it as the treasury of his love for us from which we can draw to answer that love. He knows we are tempted toward lesser loves even while we are living respectably and attending church. Like the impressive Ephesian church, we can look good on the outside, even as we are well on the way to losing our first love (Revelation 2:1-4).

The definitive Pentecost event concludes with Peter interpreting what this infilling of the Holy Spirit means to those gathered. The first thing he says to them is "Change your hearts and lives" (Acts 2:38a). Peter is calling them—and us—to a metamorphosis, a new creation, like the transformation of a caterpillar into a butterfly. This is a deep change, a re-creation of or in the heart, a strengthening and inflaming of our heart for God, the one who first loved us and emptied himself for us, our divine Lover who calls us to answer his love—and we do it by opening our heart to Christ's re-creative work.

Prayer

Dear Christ, changer and re-creator of the human heart, I hear you inviting me to open my heart to your gift of still a new creation. You know me better than I know myself. You know where the heart of my Christian living may have blockage. You know if my motivation is mixed or my life compromised. You know if I've lost my first Love and why. I pray for healing followed by re-creation where you have revealed a blockage in my heart. If you have not revealed it, or if I have not been receptive, please open my eyes over the next few days, so that I can see where I need heart change and by your Spirit ask for it. I pray this prayer in the name of Jesus. Amen.

TUESDAY THE FOURTH WEEK OF LENT
Re-Creating Our Body

*Scripture for Reflection: Genesis 1:26-31;
I Corinthians 6:12-20*

Our relationship to our bodies is one of the most misunderstood aspects of holy living among large numbers of Christians. Some religions portray the body as inherently evil and our life on earth as consumed with subduing, punishing, or escaping it. From this perspective, salvation is our soul being freed from our body in eternity. Other religions deify the body, as if what is physical is the only real thing. The Christian faith says it's all real and all good, the physical and the spiritual.

Echoing the words of Creator God in early Genesis, Christians affirm the goodness of all God's creation (Genesis 1:31). When God created humans, however, he did something different: he formed them in his own image, "in the divine image" (1:27); he breathed into them "the breath of life" (2:7). They became embodied souls, not souls trapped in an evil body, but souls at home in a good body.

Almost from the start, those religions that honor the soul and despise the body have tried to influence Christian thinking and practice. The influence has been seen in Christians who think they are honoring God by punishing their bodies or ignoring the health of their bodies in other ways. They may damage their bodies by their own drivenness, their lack of body care and needed rest, or they may overeat or feed other addictions. Medical science has proven that all of these abuses damage bodily and even mental health. They are also a Christian heresy in practice: God's good creation, which we are commanded to nurture and care for (Genesis 2:15), is God's gift, and it is all good. But it is one thing to believe in your mind that the world and your body are God's gifts to be treasured and cared for; it is another to treat them accordingly. Perhaps our behavior demonstrates what we really believe (James 1:22-25). As Jesus says, we can hear and pretend to accept his words, but the truth is proven by our actions (Luke 6:46-49).

Caring for our bodies requires honoring our need for proper nutrition. The measure for this is "enough" not "as much as I can." A Christian writer who struggled with overeating found a very helpful guideline for herself: "When I sit down to eat, I imagine that the whole world is sitting at that table, and there is a limited amount of food for us all. I realize that millions of those at the table are undernourished or starving. How much food do I take?" The issue becomes heart compassion rather than legalistic discipline. We must also be aware and concerned that nutritious food is far more difficult to find and afford in poorer areas. We should recognize this exclusion and pray that we as a nation take steps to address it, maybe even that we do something ourselves to help rectify this unholy human rights disparity.

Another aspect of body care is exercise. Whereas food gives the body needed nutrition, exercise provides the necessary utilization of the nutrition to keep the body fit and healthy. Exercise used to come almost naturally with a person's day—for example, the necessity of extended walking to get to where you needed to go. These days, however, it's far more often something you need to plan and make time to do. Consider also how the labor-saving devices that have been flooding the marketplace for decades have taken away some of the exertions that kept us trimmer! We need not join the cult of those who have become obsessed—and sometimes almost addicted—to the profile of a perfect body-preening that draws attention. Nurturing a healthy body because our bodies are God's creation and gift, however, is a part of our calling as followers of Jesus.

The apostle Paul tells us that our bodies are "the temple of the Holy Spirit" and we are to use them "to honor God" (I Corinthians 6:19-20). He says, "I hope...that Christ's greatness will be seen in my body" (Philippians 1:20). Was Paul's body perfect? Undoubtedly not, just as none of our bodies is perfect in every way. But they are perfect for honoring and serving God. No disciple's body, no matter how impaired by injury or limitation, is in such a condition as to prevent the overflow of love for God.

George Marshall was bandmaster of a Salvation Army church band in England during the early and mid-twentieth century. A coal miner by occupation, his legs were crushed in a devastating mining accident, and he lived in a wheelchair for the rest of his life. What we remember him for is the music he wrote and we sang, music that came out of bodily impairment and pain and transformed it into acceptance, understanding, and even joy.

Prayer
Dear Christ, my Creator, if there are any ways I have not used my body to honor you, if I have not cared for my body or if I have even abused it, I ask your forgiveness. I ask you to take the body I now have, in whatever condition it is in, and re-create it toward a better health as I do my part to cooperate with you. I ask this in your Name. Amen.

WEDNESDAY THE FOURTH WEEK OF LENT
Re-Creating Our Spiritual Practice

Scripture for Reflection: Psalm 46; Romans 12:1-2

Life lived at an increasingly rapid pace challenges the depth and integrity of our spiritual practice. How many spaces in our week do we have when we can be still and know that God really is God (Psalm 46:10)? Do we ever pause in the midst of the bustle to look for God? Or suddenly feel God's pull in an unplanned or perhaps uncomfortable direction? Simply put, in light of our very busy and largely overburdened lives, how can we allow God to be a guide and participant in our day—or to begin with, simply be a real presence?

Along with the fast pace, there is another threat to our spiritual focus: frequent distractions. We live in a media culture committed to keeping our minds on something else. Their business and their financial success depend on the multiple manufactured distractions they generate. I am not speaking of highly informative and moving series such as a Ken Burns documentary or a Christian program that deals in a helpful way with important matters of Christian life and witness. I am talking, rather, about the mass market of entertainment for entertainment's sake alone—that is, the industry that manufactures escapism. This industry claims to have the antidote to the exhaustion created by our frenzied days. It presents an alternate world which, in the final analysis, does not re-create or even refresh us. It only distracts us for the immediate time being. We followers of Jesus do not need an alternate world; we need spiritual practices that help us engage the world we live in.

Perhaps the most pervasive distractive force across our land is social media. It began innocently and with good intentions to connect us. It now enables us to access friends and family who otherwise are more difficult or expensive to link up with. It is instantaneous and cheap. But it has also become a means of spewing hatred and pushing people further apart.

There is yet another aspect of it that is or can be a threat to a focused spiritual life: its aggressive ubiquity. It begs to be our ever-present companion and informer. I have observed that mobile phone users tend to have their phones with them at all times, and when they don't, they have absent-mindedly forgotten to bring them. If it rings, bings, dings, sings, or vibrates at any given time, the person wonders who or what is trying to get in touch. He will often (always?) interrupt an otherwise good conversation or deep thought about something of consequence or anything good enough to beg no interruption—just to see what the call, text, message, posting, etc. is all about. We rationalize answering because "it might be something important or something I need to know right now to be up-to-date or well-informed." And we are conditioned to answer or feel guilty about not answering precisely because we are losing, or have lost, our ability to focus. I know this as someone who has sometimes answered for no good reason or out of curiosity simply because of…what? Boredom? Fear of missing something? Hoping for some unexpected good news? The world has come to us, dumping everything on us, drowning us with exponentially more information than is helpful or even decent. Why do we answer?

If we stop and consider our frantic busyness, our constant disruptions, the assault of the entertainment industry on our ability to deal with the real issues of our lives, and the overwhelming invasiveness of social media, we may begin to see (if we haven't already) that our spiritual practices are at best being challenged and at worst adversely affected. These forces thrive when we fail to focus on the specifics of living as disciples of Jesus and on submitting ourselves daily to Christ's re-creative work in the fiber of our faith.

The foundation of this re-creative work is our intimacy with God. I have found it helpful to begin my day in quiet contemplation, praying "Be still and know that I am God" (Psalm 46:10) before I begin to praise, share concerns, bring my petitions, or read my Bible. And then I try to make it a point at certain times during the day to ask God what he's up to and how I can be present with him over the course of my day. (If you need more help with the specifics of your spiritual practices, please consult someone whose wisdom you trust.)

Prayer
Dear Lord, still my soul each morning so that I can allow myself to be present with you at the day's beginning. And help me then to carry with me that day the atmosphere of your presence and the agenda of your will. Help me to live my day as the extension of my communion with you, and my words and actions as an extension of my worship. I pray this through your Spirit and in the name of my ever-present Christ. Amen.

THURSDAY THE FOURTH WEEK OF LENT
RE-CREATING OUR PURPOSE

Scripture for Reflection: Mark 8:27-38;
Luke 18:28-30; Matthew 28:18-20

Yesterday's devotional was an invitation to adopt spiritual practices to help us nurture our intimacy with God and our awareness of him over the course of our day. Today we look at the purposing of our lives. What is our destiny, our mission on this earth, the thing our spiritual practices enable us to fulfill? In short, what is our purpose as followers of Jesus.

Jesus, of course, is our model. He has one destiny engraved on his heart. And he chooses it with all the courage his soul can muster. There are many good things he could have decided to do, many directions he could have gone, many other choices he could have made. But he makes the one choice, does the one thing, pursues the one mission. He does the will of his Father in heaven. He finds his destiny.

At first, his disciples are caught up in the romance of what they think is Jesus' destiny. At Caesarea Philippi, Peter boldly claims that Jesus is the Christ, the Anointed of God who has come to free and restore Israel. Jesus with his disciples is to lead the way in this fulfillment of prophecy. He indicates that what Peter says is true. But he has more to say. He goes on to tell them that he will suffer many things, be widely rejected by the religious leaders, and then he will be killed and after three days, rise from the dead. The disciples are stunned, their hopes stymied. Peter is so crushed he grabs Jesus, scolds him, and starts to correct him. Jesus says to him, "Get behind me, Satan. You are not thinking God's thoughts but human thoughts."

Jesus then calls others to join his disciples and proceeds to tell them: All who want to come after me must say no to themselves, take up their cross, and follow me. All who want to save their lives will lose them. But all who lose their lives because of me and because of the good news will save them.

Why would people gain the whole world but lose their lives?

Jesus knows that to give us his life is to give us his death. His death validates his life. It proves how dead serious he is in how he lives it. To have refused his death would have been to apologize for his life. It isn't until he is on a cross and near death that he says with profound truth, "It is finished." Not over with, but completed, fulfilled. The whole purpose of his earthly life.

It is no accident that after telling his small circle of disciples about his impending suffering and death, Jesus gathers more people and explains the larger truth of that suffering and death. Each of them—and all of us, for that matter—have to come to terms with the death we bring to our death. We're not sure when Jesus died to himself, but once it started he died every day to the very end. When did it start for you and me? It started, or will start, when we allow Jesus to begin the new creation, the re-purposing of our lives toward intimacy with God and living the life of Jesus in the world—from here on and until we finally surrender our earthly life for eternal life.

The message and the life of Jesus are addressed to a world of people who have lost their way because they have fashioned an alternate life for themselves. We were created for true intimacy with God and with one another, and we have instead fashioned a distant, legalistic God and pursued casual, self-serving relationships with others. We were given Jesus' life as the model for our living, and instead we have watered down or "spiritualized" his teachings and avoided taking the uncomfortable and courageous action steps he calls us to take. Jesus unquestionably calls us to love our enemies, and we still think we're supposed to have enemies and hate them. He calls us to discover him in "the least of these," and we allow ourselves only condescending charity toward the poor and marginalized. Jesus points us to the beautiful, small, and the magnificent large details of God's creation as if they were treasures to be nurtured and preserved, and we have selfishly and unthinkingly exploited them.

The divine Christ came in the form of Jesus to re-create us in all these dimensions and more. Our Creator and Re-Creator is very much alive today. Where do you want to start? What are you willing to die to and live for, in order to welcome the next phase of your re-creation?

Prayer
Dear Christ, Re-Creator, I offer you this for you to re-create in my life:_____. I want to take this step to grow closer to who I really am, and I ask for your grace to enable me to be more like Jesus. In his name I pray, Amen.

FRIDAY THE FOURTH WEEK OF LENT
Re-Creating Our Spiritual Family

Scripture for Reflection: John 15:1-8

Church congregations sometimes have homecomings. Homecomings are opportunities to remember what this particular spiritual family has meant to its members over the years. They are attended by church members and former members. Together, those assembled thank God for how he has blessed their church family over the years. High moments and poignant memories are recalled, and usually some tough and uncertain times when God brought the congregation through disagreements, difficulties, and perhaps even some internal fights, to a place of healing or resolution. Maybe the healing never really came, and the pain went underground, but such failures would probably not be talked about at the homecoming, except in whispers.

There is much to be learned about how reconciliation within a congregation can take place, but that is far more than we can address in this brief meditation. My purpose of this meditation is to look to Scripture to see what it is above all else that tells us *what the church actually is.* This is the starting point for whatever else in the church we may address. My observation is that some (many?) Christians *don't* really know what this church of which they are members is, or they have forgotten. It's easy to imagine this is the case today, because a great deal of the New Testament addresses early misunderstandings of what makes the church the church. When there is ignorance or avoidance of why there *is* a church in the first place, it is hard to address problems in a congregation.

There is only one place to begin, and that is to ask and answer the question "Who is Christ?" He is the Creator, and, as we said in Sunday's meditation, he is also the Re-Creator. Another way of saying it is to say he has been Creator since the beginning, and he still is. And that applies to all Creation. Those beautiful, lush green trees I see out my window this morning represent—actually *are*—part of Christ's new creation. Without Christ, they don't exist.

The same goes for the church. The church is God's re-creation of a people made possible by Christ in the form of Jesus of Nazareth. Christ became a human (Jesus) who gathered some disciples to form a church and then to give his life to them, and through them to the world. Consider the multiple ways the New Testament portrays how essential Christ is to the church:

- Jesus the Christ said, "I am the vine; you [his followers—i.e. the church] are the branches. If you remain in me and I in you, then you will produce much fruit [for the kingdom of God]. Without me you can do nothing" (John 15:5).

- The apostle Paul says the church "must be rooted and built up in him [Christ]" (Colossians 2:7a). Speaking to the Corinthian church, he says that Christ is the only foundation [of the church] (I Corinthian 3:11).

- Using a similar metaphor, Paul calls Christ "the cornerstone" of the church, the stone that is necessary to hold the building (the church) together (Ephesians 2:20).

- Paul also says that "Christ is the head of the church, that is, the savior of the body" (Ephesians 5:23b).

- The church, in fact, says Paul, is "one body in Christ," and because of that, "individually we belong to each other" (Romans 12:5). All Christians (whether they know it or not) are a part of the one Body of Christ (I Corinthians 12:12).

Taken all together, this means that the church (your congregation) is only alive to the extent it is drawing life and sustenance from Christ, grounding and rooting its decision-making and action in Christ, living in obedience to him, and relying on his uniting strength. Does your own faith community look at itself through this lens? If they did, what would be revealed?

Rembrandt was once asked how he knew when a painting had been completed. He answered, "When it fulfills the full intention of the artist."

Your congregation, your spiritual family, is a canvas on which Christ, the Master Painter, is in the process of painting a community called church. He knows what the finished product will look like. What can you and your faith community do to make his masterpiece come to life?

Prayer

Dear Lord, I lift up my spiritual family to you, asking that you re-create us as your Body, your people, through the sanctifying power of the Holy Spirit. Help me to see my church through your eyes, to pray for her, and to give myself to her as you gave yourself to us. Through Christ, the Lord and Head of the church, I pray. Amen.

SATURDAY THE FOURTH WEEK OF LENT
Re-Creating Our World

Scripture for Reflection: Psalm 145:9-21; Matthew 25:31-46

As with the church, Christ is asking for our help in re-creating the world. He needs our help because he created us free. We are free to hurt this planet and to exploit and disadvantage other people—both of which the human race has done. Christ doesn't just come along and fix the damage we've done so that we can continue our destructive course. He allows us to reap what we've sown, but what he really and so deeply wants is for us to help him re-create his world.

Consider first *the world of nature.* Vincent Van Gogh once said that when he felt a need for "religion," he went outside in the night to paint the stars. (See his captivating painting "Starry Night.") If this soul could see the divine in the stars, perhaps all of us followers of Christ could learn to see God and cherish the miracle of his creativity in the world around us. How can we really cherish it, however, if we do nothing to fight the destruction of it? Here is what I wrote on the subject in *Following the Rabbi Jesus: The Christian's Forgotten Calling* (pgs. 114-115):

> Wendel Berry and others who spend time looking at our relationship with the world we inhabit make a distinction between seeing our planet primarily as a place to appropriate for our own ambitions and seeing it primarily as a place to call home. They wonder if those who see our planet as an environment to be exploited and despoiled are winning out over those who see it as a world to be treasured and cared for. If you follow

the money, the weather, and the pollution, the answer by far would be the first group. A growing body of scientific study suggests that, short of major changes in lifestyle and major intervention in practices that do serious harm to the planet, we are headed toward one environmental crisis after another.

Christians seem divided on the question. Some talk and act as if they have no doctrine of Creation. They think this world is going to be trashed anyway, so they let it be raped while they sit around waiting for the Rapture. I remember occasionally hearing disparaging remarks about liberal, tree-hugging Christians. Fortunately, the tide appears to be changing, as more and more churches are rediscovering that this planet is God's miracle that he asks us to cherish and a rich resource he expects us to manage responsibly.

However we think God will bring about "a new heaven and a new earth" (Revelation 21:1a), it hardly seems a defensible attitude to say it doesn't matter if we trash the creation God has gifted us with. After all, he's going to create a totally new one. Right? We can speed it along by making this present earth unlivable. But if we do this to God's present gift of creation, do you think he would trust us with another? I suspect stewardship of this earth is far more important to God than we may think! In fact, it is participation in Christ's re-creation of our planet, and it is part of our calling as citizens of this planet.

Let's transition to the world of people. Why do we fear people who look and act differently? Why do we build walls or draw lines to keep us apart from them? Why do we create social and political systems that keep people who are not white in a more vulnerable position socially, educationally, economically, and medically? Why do we deny the reality of systemic racism?

Jesus seems to have the most empathy toward those who are the victims of our exclusion. He calls us to treat them as if they were Jesus (Matthew 25:21-46). His life lived mostly among the poorer classes of his day calls into question the systemic racism that keeps the marginalized as marginalized as possible. How then do we look at what Jesus calls us to do in a world so sinfully divided as ours? How do we participate in Christ's re-creation of the world of people where all racial and ethnic groups are not treated equally?

The answer of Jesus is to love our neighbors as ourselves (Matthew 19:19). That's not just the person next door; it's the person we all too often try not to see. It includes all races and ethnicities, even our enemies (5:43-44). Here is the poignant way Frederick Buechner describes this way of loving:

> If we are to love our neighbors, before doing anything else we must *see* our neighbors. With our imagination as well as our eyes, that is to say like artists, we must see not just their faces but the life behind and in their faces. Here it is love that is the frame we see them in (*Listening to Your Life*).

Christ is active in the world. He is very much alive, and he invites us to partner with him in re-creating the endangered natural world and the broken human world by breaking down the delusions and lies and by taking action.

Prayer
Dear Christ, show me how to partner with you in re-creating your world, and give me the courage and grace to take action. In your Name, Amen.

SUNDAY THE FIFTH WEEK OF LENT
Jesus Uniting Us

Scripture for Reflection: John 17:20-23

We can thank Paul for teaching us that the church is like a human body made up of its different parts. We are those parts, working together to enable the church to fulfill its purpose (chapters 12 of Romans and I Corinthians). God has made Christ the head of this body, and when the body follows the head, it expresses "the fullness of Christ" himself (Ephesians 1:22-23). The gifts are given to members of the body to equip the church for service and to build up the members of the body (4:12). And we grow, joined and held together by Christ, the head, as we build ourselves up in love and make our important contributions (4:16). Sounds wonderful, but as Paul learned quickly, it doesn't always work to perfection, because of both our own imperfections and our sinfulness. Paul himself acknowledges this again and again in his letters (see, for example, Romans 16:17-18; I Corinthians 1:10-13; II Thessalonians 3:6-11).

Divisions in a congregation can center on any number of issues, and they often hide the real causes. Something painful may have happened years ago between individuals, families, or other groups in the congregation, and the matter was never resolved. The repressed anger or hurt may now raise its head in the form of another unrelated issue. We may wonder why each of the parties is so immovable, so stubborn about their positions on a particular decision that needs to be made, and the reason is that there is a different battle being fought, on a deeper level. When this is the case and the sides won't let themselves find agreement or peace, someone must speak truth, and lead the persons or groups on the painful, but healing journey back to the original misunderstanding or breach or sin. In such a place Christ can speak his healing words and the healing can begin—I say begin, because the healing does not usually come instantaneously. There is ongoing work to be done, because the demons of divisiveness do not give up easily. The old hurts and hatreds may be stirred at some other point. Christian pastors and caring brothers and sisters who see deeper will be needed to come alongside to represent the healing of Christ.

Apart from these kinds of complex situations, there are a number of other matters over which there are differences which could erupt in a divisive way. Consider first the matter of race and ethnicity. It has often been said that the churches at worship on a Sunday morning are in sum the most segregated gatherings in America. To be sure, almost 400 years of black oppression and exclusion have shaped the view of many whites toward blacks as "the other," the lesser, even as a threat to our (white) American civilization. Hispanics, as well, are often looked upon with suspicion, as the ones bringing drug cartels and other undesirable baggage into "our country." Regrettably, such attitudes and fears within a congregation undermine its unity in Christ. And there is the matter of economic disparity in a congregation. Just the difference in respective lifestyles and living conditions may create a level of cultural discomfort and constraint. Poorer members may feel that their voice is not taken as seriously as those with high or higher incomes who account for more of the financial giving—even though the lower-income givers may actually tithe a larger percentage of their earnings. Money brings influence, and sometimes the pastoral leaders of a congregation are unfairly swayed by those whose giving comprises a lion's share of the church's financial resources. And finally, members of a congregation may be divided by their political views, each group claiming their political party best represents the values of Christian faith.

How does a congregation deal with these differences within the Body of Christ when they become divided, whether those divides are expressed as overt issues that break into the open, or instead, remain as disabling currents under the surface? In Christ, God loved the whole world all the way to his own death. He loved everyone and everything he created (John 3:16). In his eyes, no race or ethnicity has any claim to superiority or special status. He says the person or group claiming to be the greater is not, because true greatness is hidden in those who take the place of the least (Luke 22:24-27). Nor does any person of wealth in the congregation have any God-given right to wield greater power in the Body of Christ (Luke 12:15-21; James 1:9-11). According to Jesus, wealth is a lurking danger for those who possess it, and it should keep them on their knees. The church of Jesus is a level playing field when it comes to status. Personal wealth or the lack thereof should not affect the respect between members in the Body of Christ.

The same principle applies when it comes to political allegiance. Some seem to think they have a revelation that God has endowed one particular political party over all others as the sole bearer of his will for their country. Once that decision is made, then those who prefer a different party are often seen as misguided or sadly deluded. Members of Jesus' church need to be able to meet together "showing honor to each other" because they "love each other like family members" (Romans 12:10). This certainly includes sharing differing political allegiances without demeaning or attacking. In the polarized environment of our day, such an approach would be a genuine miracle—and a strong witness to the world of the church as a place of Christ's love transcending differences.

Another possible area of division relates to Christian belief itself. One person can read Scriptural teaching on a particular subject one way, and another person can interpret it differently. The area of difference may have to do with doctrine. For example, how we understand the Bible as the inspired Word of God, or how literally we should interpret some of the radical teachings of Jesus in the Gospels, or how we see the relationship of Father, Son, and Holy Spirit in the Trinity. There will also be some differences in how we see the church in relation to the individual Christian, and how we believe authority and power should work in the church. There will also be some differences relating to how we see certain ethical issues from a Christian perspective. In all these areas of Christian belief, setting up battle stations for proving or defending one's interpretation of Scripture will only create divisions that hurt the unity and witness of the Body. Again, when such a division in views emerges, the way forward is to create a setting where members listen to one another and speak truthfully in love (Ephesians 4:15) while each one is given the opportunity to share her position and relate it to Scripture. Otherwise, suspicions and distrust will creep in, and some members will distance themselves from others. How can a body live in such a state? It can only pretend to live.

The church is our spiritual home, and church gatherings are like family meals. As the family gathers in love and prays in unity, transformation happens. Hidden hurts are healed. Racial, ethnic, socio-economic, and political divides are overcome. And differences in what each family member hears Scripture saying to him draws the family closer together for better understanding. To the extent that family members actually listen to one another and humble themselves before God while affirming the presence of Christ in the Word of God, to that extent they are indeed the Body of Christ.

Jesus the Christ said that he was in his disciples as his heavenly Father was in him, to the end that they (the church) would be made perfectly one (John 17:23). Jesus goes on to say, "Then the world will know that you (the Father) sent me and that you have loved them just as you loved me." When we allow Christ to unite us, with all our differences, disagreements, and disparities, we learn that opening ourselves to one another frees us to be one in love. The world takes notice. And we find ourselves in a better position and greater readiness to open ourselves to that world, which is our ultimate calling.

Prayer
Heavenly Father, thank you for uniting your church in Christ, just as you united those first followers in Jesus the incarnate Christ. I confess that I have not always lived in that oneness with my spiritual brothers and sisters. I have sometimes distanced them by my judging, my arrogance, and by my withheld love. I ask you, Lord, to give me discernment beyond my shortsightedness, openness to the diversity around me, and acceptance of the differences among my fellow followers of Christ. Help me to be your unifier and a part of your reconciling work in the church and in the world around me. I ask this in the name of our uniting Lord, Jesus the Christ. Amen.

MONDAY THE FIFTH WEEK OF LENT
Suffering Together

Scripture for Reflection: I Peter 4:12-5:13

It may sound strange to say that Christ unites us in suffering. Don't people come together in groups and communities for enjoyment, security, and personal satisfaction? Painful things may happen in such bodies, but those occasions were not part of the group's intention. They are usually problems that need to be worked through. As we saw in yesterday's meditation, the same is true for the church. If a congregation does not address the internal problems that engender disunity and polarization, the Body of Christ will be crippled.

Today we are looking at something quite different. The apostle Paul speaks of his desire "to know Christ and the power of his resurrection *and the fellowship of sharing in his sufferings…*" (Philippians 3:10a, NIV, italics added). He adds to this: "becoming like [Christ] in his death, and so, somehow, to attain to the resurrection from the dead" (v. 10b-11). What *is* this "fellowship of sharing in Christ's sufferings"?

To answer this, we must know what Jesus' sufferings were. They did not begin on the cross. He was misunderstood, maligned, and mistreated during his whole three-year ministry. Like an Old Testament prophet, he paid the price of his prophetic integrity. His blistering critique of the religious establishment and the wealthy's exploitation of the poor, his seeming threat to the Roman social order, and the unsettling messianic claims all merged to profile him as dangerous—a considerable inconvenience to be done away with. The cross itself was not the beginning of the suffering; it was the elevation of it to redemptive proportions, for which the trials of his three-year mission had prepared him.

This fact is important to recognize because if we focus only on Jesus' redemptive suffering on the cross while ignoring the suffering of those three years, we miss some of the important lessons of his life. Jesus showed us that being his disciples would inevitably bring suffering in a world threatened by his radical love. We are tempted, however, to believe that Jesus did all the suffering on the cross and to dismiss any part that suffering has in our own Christian lives: "Jesus paid it all" so we don't have to pay any price at all. A Christian life of convenience. On the contrary, to be a Christian, a disciple of Jesus, is an assignment to suffering. Not just for some unfortunate members of our congregation, for all of us. Paul tells the Corinthian congregation that they are *partners together* in both suffering and comfort (II Corinthians 1:7).

This suffering is not just any suffering, caused by accident or our own mistakes or stupidity. It is suffering that comes because we are sincerely seeking to live the life Jesus lived and taught us to live with sufficient credibility to engender some of the same kind of opposition, exclusion, and deprivation suffered by Jesus. Living by our Lord's command to love God with all our hearts and to love our neighbors as ourselves (Mark 12:29-31) comes with the price of personal suffering. The word compassion literally means to "suffer with someone." Love not willing to suffer is not compassion. Suffering comes with the territory of being a follower of Jesus.

We do not, however, suffer alone. We suffer with other members of the Body of Christ (I Corinthians 12:26) and in that shared suffering is great strength. Christ's church is a suffering church, comprised of members who continue the suffering of Christ, not because his suffering was not adequate for our salvation—it was—but because his church is called to point to his suffering love by her own suffering for the world's salvation.

An old Hasidic maxim says: "Our hearts must break before the Word can fall in." We could add: Our hearts must break before another person can fall into God. Over the years, some Christians have been willing to make the ultimate sacrifice and let their hearts break for someone else with the sacrifice of their own lives. The year of this writing, when the coronavirus was ravaging Italy, a humble village priest named Don Giuseppe Berardelli contracted the virus and because of his vulnerable age was given a respirator that was purchased specifically for him by one of his parishioners. He refused to take it and instead insisted it go to a younger patient who was struggling to breathe, a person the priest did not know. The priest died soon after. (See John 15:13.) But he left a life that pointed undeniably to Jesus.

The church's suffering is the soil to grow new seedlings for God's kingdom. A church that attracts with a religion of comfort is a church without kingdom soil. A church united in its suffering for the sake of the world will be fertile ground for the transformation of lives.

Prayer

Dear suffering Lord, empower me with the grace of giving myself to others, even when I am misunderstood, maligned, or mistreated. Please grant me the grace and courage of a Father Berardelli to put others before myself. Help me to reach out to my brothers and sisters in Christ where I worship and serve, to share their and my suffering, so that Christ can bring us closer together in his love strength. I pray this in your name and for the sake of your kingdom. Amen.

TUESDAY THE FIFTH WEEK OF LENT
Singing Together

Scripture for Reflection: Psalm 95:1-7; Ephesians 5:18b-21; Colossians 3:16-17

If Christ unites his church (his Bride) in her suffering (yesterday's meditation), he *lifts* her through her singing. Whether the songs she sings are expressions of gratitude and love to God, calls to Christlike action, or spiritual meditations, they all are grounded in the gifts and graces of God. These gifts and graces have little to nothing to do with worldly success and powerful influence in the fields of finance, business, politics, or religion. They have to do with considering "everything as loss in comparison with the spiritual value of knowing Christ Jesus [our] Lord" (Philippians 3:8). One could compose a hymn of sorts centered on hope or gratitude for material prosperity, personal recognition, self-love, or unlimited freedom, but it would have no place in Christian worship. Christian singing lifts us to God, no matter our situation in life.

We don't know exactly how God created everything, but maybe he sang it into existence. It certainly appears we are a part of his creation that can sing back to him. So much of the Bible can and has been sung. The Psalms, for example. The psalmist invites the whole congregation to sing their gratitude to God:

> Come. Let's sing out loud to the Lord!
> Let's raise a joyful shout to the rock of our salvation!
> Let's come before him with thanks!
> Let's shout songs of joy to him! (Psalm 95:1-2)

Our singing together is part of the unique way we humans

communicate with God.

It is also one of the ways the Spirit of God binds us together as the Body of Christ. In his letter to the Ephesian church, Paul admonishes the members to "speak to each other with songs, hymns, and spiritual songs" while they "sing and make music to the Lord in [their] hearts" and "always give thanks to God the Father in everything in the name of our Lord Jesus Christ… submit[ting] to each other out of respect for Christ" (Ephesians 5:19-20). These are all ways, in combination, to be filled with the Spirit (v. 18b). What is intriguing about these words is that they blend communicating with God and communicating with each other.

This book of meditations is being written while the coronavirus is infecting hundreds of thousands but has also taken the lives of tens of thousands in the USA. One of the most important protective requirements has been social distancing. Churches that remained open often faced tragic consequences. Our own pastors, staff, and volunteers offered online worship, which was helpful and much appreciated. What was missing, however, was the corporate gathering, the coming together of the bodies in the Body. There is a palpableness to gathering together and letting our hearts and voices blend to sing God's praises as one Body. The screen cannot be the Body.

Ignatius, a latter first-century church leader, envisioned the church at worship as a choir of harmonious love for God and each other, singing with one voice to the Father through the Son. And our listening God, hearing the choir, perceives by the music and our good works that we are indeed members of his Son (Epistles of Ignatius, v.50-52). The whole church is one great massed choir for God, singing the gospel 24/7 around the world. In fact, the singing never ends. Father, Son, and Holy Spirit sing to one another, and we join in for eternity, when all of us will have beautiful singing voices and perfect pitch. And the song will never end.

For now, we are followers of Jesus Christ, the Pied Piper of this fallen world, luring it with his love song. Not some cheap, sentimental love song. No, a love song with pain and suffering and enormous sacrifice for his beloveds. A love song he is teaching us to sing so that we also can sing the story to the world.

Prayer
Thank you, Lord, for a faith we can sing; for the memories that sustain us, evoked by a song; for the music that pulls us from the clutches of defeat and despair; for the melodies of your miraculous grace that give us what we don't deserve and carry us where we have no capacity to go on our own; for the songs of your providence that see us through our pain and our loss to a love from which nothing can separate us.

I ask you, Lord, to tune my voice to your love and my life to Jesus, who sang to this world with his life poured out. I ask in his name. Amen.

WEDNESDAY THE FIFTH WEEK OF LENT
Drawing Closer Together

Scripture for Reflection: I Corinthians 10:24; 12:12-13:13

On Sunday, we looked at a number of issues that can divide congregations and considered how Christ invites us to address them and work toward unity. Today we look at the matter of intimacy. The word "intimate" relates to what is inmost, internal, or essential about us. Intimacy, then, is a relationship where two or more people share at a deeper level these very important things about themselves. When we look at intimacy in this way, it seems it should be a very natural part of life in the Body of Christ. As we get to know Christ, through him we also get to know our brothers and sisters in Christ.

What is shared in an intimate relationship may vary considerably. It may be what brings deep joy to the person. Or some deeply personal hope or longing. Or it may be a disabling anxiety. Or a shattering disappointment. Or some other repressed painful experience. If these "intimacies" are so important to the person—whether positively or negatively—why are they so often difficult to share with another person or group in a congregation? Aren't we brothers and sisters in Christ supposed to share our joys and sorrows (Romans 12:15)? The reason, it seems to me, is either embarrassment or fear. The embarrassment may come from insecurity about oneself and not wanting to appear too presumptuous or ridiculous. The fear may come from the threat that others will think less of us, or even despise us if the personal information is shared, especially if it is an embarrassing sin. (Some highly sensitive matters may be best shared privately with the pastor, a counselor, or a trusted, mature Christian.)

Jesus knew intimacy. He saw into people, knew their thoughts. He saw the good and the bad and loved them still, or loved them even more. In doing so he set them free to begin becoming their true selves. He also saw into himself, revealing the full range of his emotions—think of him in Gethsemane (Mark 14:32-36). Our God is a self-revealing God, and he created a self-revealing people to live openly in the garden of his creation, not hide in it (Genesis 3:8-10). We fear our secret hopes are beyond our self-confidence or capacity, so we bury them. Our sin embarrasses us, so we hide it in our shame, or we flaunt it to convince ourselves it is a perfectly natural part of being human. All such behaviors violate the message of Jesus and the character of the church which is his Body.

Christians are called to look out for each other (I Corinthians 10:24b). The very act of meeting together in fellowship is a major step in that direction. During the current coronavirus pandemic, Keitha and I and most other members of our church felt the loss of meeting together in person. We had online services, Sunday school, Bible studies, and prayer meetings, and even our discipleship group met via Zoom. We are so fortunate that current technology makes this possible. As helpful as it is, it's not the same. As one member said, "We can't hug each other." We need to be together in person.

It's true, however, that some congregations can actually meet together physically without coming together in a deeper way. It's possible to "go to church" without being the church. The unity of the Body affects the unity of worship. We cannot draw closer together as Christ's Body without "looking out for each other." Studies show that loneliness and feelings of alienation are on the rise. We Christians need to reach out to the lonely in our own church, and by doing so demonstrate to the world around us how Christ, through his church, draws us out of our painful isolation. How else will we credibly fulfill Jesus' prayer to the Father that his followers "be one," just as Father and Son are one (John 17:23)?

With eloquence and depth, the apostle Paul invites us to share life where love dominates (I Corinthians, chapter 13). In the previous chapter he explains that each of us has a gift that the church needs. We are like the parts of the human body, and just because some parts are visible, or seemingly more important—think of those whose gifts are of a more "public" nature—they are no more important than those with the less prominent gifts. The church needs all spiritual gifts. But Paul isn't finished. From that place he soars to yet another. He unveils the gift that makes the Body whole. It is, he says, the gift of God's kind of love unleashed in the Body of Christ. It is a love that breaks through the loneliness and seeks the other's good. It is so contagious that it draws notice from the world. No wonder observers of the early church often declared, "See how those Christians love one another!" So many were drawn to these small Christian groups by the way the groups drew close together in love for one another through Christ. In our day, when the church's credibility is under fire, perhaps our best hope for our own Body health and for our appeal to this desperate and needy world is for our congregations to take seriously I Corinthians, chapter 12—and seek to live out chapter 13.

Prayer

Dear Lord, thank you for allowing your body to be broken so that we can be whole. Thank you for allowing us to be part of your Body, your church, on earth. I ask you, through your Holy Spirit, to help and empower me to draw closer together with my brothers and sisters in Christ, not just the ones I naturally gravitate toward but also those I feel awkward with, foreign to, or threatened by. Enable me to be a help rather than a hindrance to the unity and witness of your Body. I ask this in the name of our unifying Jesus. Amen.

THURSDAY THE FIFTH WEEK OF LENT
Maturing Together

Scripture for Reflection: Matthew 10:25a; Acts 2:42-47

About two years ago, Keitha and I had an epiphany. Why it took so long for the revelation to land on us is a mystery. Maybe the good Lord was waiting for us to be ready. We had long known that being a Christian meant being a disciple of Jesus. A disciple of Jesus is someone who is faithful to Jesus' teaching (John 8:31), imitates him (Matthew 10:25a), loves her fellow disciples (John 13:35), her neighbors, and even her enemies (Matthew 5:43-44), and bears much fruit for God's kingdom (John 15:8). Clearly, to meet those standards requires a change of heart and life, and the process began at Pentecost where those gathered received the gift of the empowering Holy Spirit (Acts 2:37-39). It became clear to us that in comparison to what Jesus asks of us in the Gospels and what the early church suffers in the remainder of the New Testament record, the discipleship of the current church in the western world is generally anemic, with a few encouraging exceptions.

Jesus said, "I came so they [meaning us] could have life—indeed, so that they [us] could have life to the fullest" (John 10:10). If this statement is considered in isolation, it is enough to thrill us with the prospects of prosperity, and some who claim Christian faith have indeed adopted a prosperity Gospel with a sugar-daddy God. What is conveniently ignored are other words of Jesus that those who "find" their lives will also lose them, and those who lose their lives because of Jesus and the gospel will find them. These words of Jesus are found in Matthew, Mark, and Luke, coupled with this: "All who want to come after me must say no to themselves, take up their cross, and follow me" (Matthew 16:24, etc.).

Being a disciple of Jesus is first of all about losing, giving up, and dying; and then we find, receive, and live. It is not a call to private heroism. It is a call to be a part of a community of disciples who do the dying and the living together. There is no such thing as a lone disciple. We discovered that the early church, which was forbidden to meet in larger venues, met in homes and small places, and they grew exponentially throughout the Roman Empire. They were discipling groups, like the small group that Jesus discipled in person over three years. We also recalled that John and Charles Wesley, priests in an Anglican Church that did little to nurture disciples, started a spiritual revolution in the 18th century based on what they called class meetings and bands, the total focus of which was disciple making. The movement eventually evolved into the Methodist Church, which continued the class meetings for another century, before replacing them with Sunday schools. Our own denomination, The Salvation Army, is an offshoot of Methodism. We continued the class meetings, using the name holiness meetings, until we moved the holiness meetings to Sunday mornings. What had been a discipling group became Sunday worship. The discipling dimension in our denomination was greatly weakened.

Our epiphany was the realization that we needed a discipling group for our continuing maturation as Jesus' followers. A small group (no more than twelve) is small enough for the needed spiritual intimacy and large enough to allow the diversity of experience to inform and enrich each member, especially when the ages of members differ significantly. Some Christians have chosen to do discipling one on one—same gender, of course—and that allows for a higher level of trust and confidentiality, but not as much diversity of wisdom and support. When we decided to start a group, with the blessing of our pastors, we and the group we recruited decided to meet every other week, with members having a one-on-one meeting with their chosen discipleship partner during the interim week.

Our group has gradually made progress over this year and a half—even during the coronavirus pandemic which forced us to meet via Zoom! We are learning to trust each other with our spiritual hopes, joys, frustrations, failures, and progress. We share Scriptures that have blessed, challenged, or judged us. We pray for one another. We bless one another. We work at holding one another accountable for what Jesus is doing in our lives. Speaking personally, I wish I had discovered this God-given way to mature together in Christ a long time ago. (Incidentally, two members of our group have left to start another group with our blessing, and we hope for more to come!)

If you are interested in growing as a disciple of Jesus, I recommend you express your desire to your pastor and perhaps talk to others you think may have a similar desire for a discipleship group. Although such a group should have full accountability to your pastor, it should not be a "program" of your church but a meeting of Christians with a similar desire to reach, and continue to reach, greater maturity in Christ. What do you say?

LENTEN AWAKENING

Prayer

Dear Jesus, as your disciple I long to resemble you by studying your Word, listening to your Spirit, and following your path. I thank you for brother and sister disciples who desire the same. Since it is not your intention that I or they travel this spiritual journey alone, you have given us each other. Give me the confidence to reach out to them and together find a way to partner on this journey toward deeper spiritual maturity. I ask this in your name. Amen.

FRIDAY THE FIFTH WEEK OF LENT
Sharing Everything Together

Scripture for Reflection: Acts 2:42-47; 4:32-35

Some of the most striking lines in the apostle Paul's letters are found in Philippians 3:5-9. After outlining his impressive claims as a Hebrew of Hebrews—his "assets"—he says he "wrote them off as a loss for the sake of Christ." In fact, he considers "everything as loss in comparison with the superior value of knowing Christ Jesus [his] Lord." He considers what he has lost for Christ as "sewer trash, so that [he] might gain Christ and be found in him." The righteousness he now has comes only from "the faithfulness of Christ" (Philippians 3:5-9). Paul is clearly calling us to consider whatever we claim as our "assets," our accomplishments, our sources of pride as nothing. In short, there is no comparison.

In this meditation we will consider what this surrender of our assets means in our relationship to and in the church, the Body of Christ. I'll put it in the form of a direct question: How far are you willing to go in "writing off" your assets as loss in the life of the Body you are a part of?

Our culture teaches us to use our abilities to gain position, wealth, respect, so as increase our assets. Then we come to church, study the life and teachings of Jesus, and discover that he turns this way of life on its head! We've already considered some of Jesus' strange teachings. Namely, that the one who seeks the least position is the greatest and that the one who amasses wealth for its own sake has missed life. And we noticed that the people in the positions considered highly respectable were treated by Jesus with the least respect. When it come to our families, Jesus tells us that the person who loves his father, mother, son, or daughter more than he loves Jesus is not worthy of him.

Obviously, the world could not go on without people in certain positions of power and influence, or without those who manage wealth and economies, or without those whose role it is to represent and protect the better values of a culture. And we certainly need strong, healthy families. Jesus knows all this. He also knows that each of these can become the objects of our greed, and therefore our idols. He says: "Guard yourself against all kinds of greed! (Luke 12:15a). The "all kinds of greed" means that our greed can focus on just about anything: power, wealth, influence, respect—even our own family. Yes, we can covet our family by treating them as our personal possession and pride. A spouse can be considered an asset, as can children. A family can be treated as one's personal commodity.

Think now about your church family. Some Christians consider their church an asset to their life credentials, an investment in respectability, a useful commodity. They go to church but never or rarely engage in a more intimate way with what the Body of Christ is really about. In an earlier meditation, we talked about what kind of community the church is. We looked at the Greek word for church, *koinonia*, which means fellowship, a close mutual relationship, participating in partnership, making a contribution, giving a gift. Church is not someone's asset or useful commodity; it is the Body of Christ that exists to carry out Christ's purposes. If we go to church to benefit ourselves, we're using it as an asset. If we go to worship God, meet Jesus, fellowship with his followers, participate in his mission, and give of ourselves to all of that, we will be a part of the Body, benefitting ourselves only in unanticipated ways!

The church, then, is our spiritual family. We all are members of this family. We don't ask what this family can do for us; we ask what we can do for the family. We can take our cue from the early Jerusalem church in the book of Acts where these new believers formed a close family that met often for praise meetings, spiritual instruction, prayer, and family suppers; they shared everything, sold unneeded items and gave the proceeds to those in need—and by the way, the witness of this radical fellowship drew the attention of the city and "and the Lord added daily to the community those who were being saved" (See Acts 2:42-27; 4:32-35). This isn't political communism, which history has proven doesn't ultimately work. It is the miracle of what can happen when a family unites together, "one in heart and mind" (4:32). Such a Body is an eloquent, convincing witness to the world.

A question every follower of Jesus must answer is: What am I sharing with my spiritual family, my church, the Body of Christ? Whether or not we consciously answer the question, we are, in fact, answering it with our lives. We are answering it if our church is no more than a convenience or an asset to our personal profile. Or we are answering it if we are sharing ourselves and our assets, as the Body, its members, and its mission have need. If it's the latter, then we prove we truly believe that Christ has called his church to give the world a glimpse of the Kingdom of God, and that with that shining light of God's beloved community, the church's mission will bear fruit.

Prayer

Dear Jesus, I thank you for honoring me with the privilege of being a member of your church, your Body and Bride. I ask you for grace to love her and her fellow members and for unselfish strength to share with her whatever abilities and assets you've given me. In your name and for the sake of your church, I pray. Amen.

SATURDAY THE FIFTH WEEK OF LENT
Conspiring Together

Scripture for Reflection: Acts 1:1-11

It may seem strange to think of Jesus as uniting us around a conspiracy. We think of conspiracies as secret plans hatched by a group that presumably is plotting to overthrow the government or "our way of life," along with the appeal to stop them by whatever means required. The conspiracy theorists are trying to start a movement to implement major change, and they use any means available to convince others that their theory is true and action is therefore called for. They may want to bring about radical change in society by returning to some kind of idyllic past, which probably was never as idyllic as they claim. Or they may want to fulfill a social contract which a society or government promised and never sufficiently implemented. It goes without saying that what many conspiracy theorists really want is to make things better for themselves and not for other groups.

The word "conspire" literally means "to breath together." A conspiracy requires a group, large or small, that is breathing the same air of a need or intention to change things, in their minds for the better.

Is it accurate to say that the mission of Jesus is a conspiracy launched by God to change the world? I think so. There was the intention to restore the past before humanity lost its innocence, and of course, also to create a new future called the Kingdom of God. This new future would come by co-conspirators for Christ allowing the Holy Spirit to be breathed into them like a powerful wind, with the love of Christ uniting them, fire alighting on them, new tongues spoken by them, and new hearts and lives changing them. Bound together by the redemptive sacrifice of Christ and the empowering infilling of the Holy Spirit, they would set out to change the world—not to change it by government fiat but by uniting to spread Christ's gospel and live out his love convincingly and by paying the price to do it.

Jesus was a Divine Conspirator who surrounded himself with twelve co-conspirators and set out to overcome the present world order (John 16:33). He succeeded, not in a political way, but through his life-changing teaching, his radical inclusiveness, his persecution at the hands of those threatened by his gospel, his surrender to crucifixion, his victorious resurrection, and his gift of the Holy Spirit to those who chose to join the conspiracy. The Acts of the Apostles records how the conspiracy was continued by breathed-into, sanctified co-conspirator disciples of Jesus who risked their lives, suffered beatings and whippings, and sometimes death. The result? The gospel spread like wildfire. The church was a suffering, conquering movement that took the world by storm.

And then over time it started to accommodate itself to the old-world order, which reasserted itself under the guise of joining the Christ conspiracy—and instead, tamed and lamed it. The church became an accepted agency of the social order, and most Christians joined the accommodation. Over the ensuing centuries, there have been many individuals and reform movements that have refused the compromise and embraced the conspiracy. Their deep commitment to Christ stands as a beckoning call to us all.

Can we be co-conspirators with Christ in our day? I'm convinced we can. I'm thinking of a teenage conspirator that the world became acquainted with at the year of this writing. Her conspiracy is to save the world's environment. I have no idea if she is a Christian or is affiliated with any other formal religion. I do believe, however, that Christ, through whom this universe and everything in it was created and through whom it all continues to exist (Colossians 1:15-17), weeps when he sees us trash and abuse this extraordinary, interconnected planet of his. Greta Thunberg does not hesitate to weep, shout, stand before anyone and any world body, make any sacrifice, to plead on behalf of a planet she has evidence to believe we are gradually destroying.

What if we tired of a shallow Christianity of accommodation, compromise, and cowardness and became gospel conspirators together with the passion of a Greta Thunberg? What if we allowed ourselves to begin breathing sanctifying Spirit together? What if we invited Christ to unite us in a conspiracy to free a sinful world living in illusions and lies and to offer real hope? And what if we allowed our lives to give definition to the love-grounded, grace-filled life of Jesus. What if we became world-transforming followers of Jesus?

So here we are, on the cusp of Holy Week and Easter Sunday. As we prepare to follow Jesus the last week of his life, let us keep in mind that we are invited to be co-conspirators in his world-transforming revolution. We have the privilege of dying to ourselves, coming alive in him, and following his grace-filled, love-giving way of life.

Prayer
Thank you, Lord, for inviting me to be a part of your Divine Conspiracy to save and transform the world. Give me courage to take my place and do my part to trust the power of your love and to stand against the enemies of your extraordinary Kingdom. I pray in your Name. Amen.

HOLY WEEK
Walking the Last Week with Jesus

We have arrived at the most significant week of Jesus' life: his last on earth. I invite you to be present with Jesus on that final stage of his journey, to observe closely what he says and does. He still has so much to teach us about himself and our calling to live as his disciples. And there is so much to grasp—and to gain—as we move toward the week's climax and try to take in the enormity of Jesus' suffering and the universal benefit of his crucifixion.

I have mentioned before that as I write these pages, the world is suffering from the coronavirus pandemic. People around the world are getting sick and hundreds of thousands are dying. People are scared. We are fighting an enemy hidden from the naked eye. The best preventive for us all is isolation, but most of us are not used to such extended confinements. We become distracted and bored, fearful, even paranoid.

Considering the last week of his life, what does Jesus offer us in the times of our uncertainty and even despair? He is facing his own enemies, and he knows this week will end with his own horrible death. Watching him this last week of his earthly life, we will see courage, humility, compassion, authenticity, and hope. He offers us, his disciples, these same gifts:

- Courage to act when fairness and judgment demand it

- Humility before God and each other

- Compassion for all who suffer and lose loved ones

- Authenticity as his followers, even if it calls us to suffer, and

- Sure hope in our future with Christ, come what may.

Prayer

Dear Jesus of the human road, as we walk with you this final week of your earthly life, open our eyes to see, our ears to hear, our minds to grasp, and our hearts to be grasped by your every act of compassion and by the saving scope of your suffering and death. We ask this in your name, our worthy Savior and Lord. Amen.

PALM SUNDAY THE SIXTH WEEK OF LENT
Riding a Donkey

Scripture for Reflection: Luke 19:28-44

Today Jesus enters Jerusalem on a borrowed donkey. We have traditionally called this event "the Triumphal Entry." There are, indeed, shouts of joy, as if a conquering hero is entering the sacred city: "Blessings on the king who comes in the name of the Lord." Clothes and palm branches are thrown on the road, as if welcoming royalty. Lest these words be mistaken for cheers for a conquering military or even political leader, they are followed by more tranquil words referring to a nonpolitical spiritual realm: "Peace in heaven and glory in the highest heavens."

The words are reminiscent of Zechariah's prophecy: "Rejoice greatly, Daughter Zion./ Sing aloud, Daughter Jerusalem./ Look, your king will come to you./ He is righteous and victorious./ He is humble and riding on an ass,/ on a colt, the offspring of a donkey" (Zech. 9:9). This humility, riding on a donkey, will "cut off the chariot from Ephraim and the warhorse from Jerusalem." The warring bow will be replaced by "peace to the nations," and this triumph of peace "will stretch from sea to sea" (9:10). Jesus' disciples don't understand what the words of the vocal bystanders mean. The Gospel of John tells us that it won't become clear to them till after Jesus is glorified (12:16).

I am intrigued by the choice of a donkey. There's an old mountain road in Northeast Georgia we like to walk. One stretch of it passes through a beautiful valley with grassy pastureland. A couple of years ago the owners added a donkey to one section of the larger grazing area. For reasons we don't understand, they named him Bunny. On occasion, before starting out on one of our hikes, we remember to bring a carrot for Bunny. This one time he seemed especially friendly and remained a few extra moments. When I stroked and patted his back for the first time, I was surprised at how solid and strong the body of this humble animal felt. And then I remembered that the early Catholic missionaries in the rough western mountains of North America, when they traveled far to visit mission stations, chose to ride a donkey over the unforgiving terrain instead of a larger but more fragile horse.

Jesus, however, doesn't actually own a donkey, nor do his disciples. So, he sends them into town to borrow one, a colt that has never been ridden, as Zechariah said. They find the colt, and when they untie it, the owners ask them what they think they're doing. The disciples explain: "Its master needs it." Strangely, the owners accept the explanation. They are the owners, but Jesus is the beast's master. He is a master who owns nothing and has to ask. Jesus, the humblest of human beings.

Jesus rides into Jerusalem on this borrowed beast of burden, not a well-appointed white stallion. He represents the power of an enduring spiritual kingdom, not an earthly empire that will inevitably fall. Empires both secular and religious govern by fear, and when the fear is no longer there, or no longer works, the empire collapses. The power of Jesus is the power of self-giving love, and nothing could be more foreign, or dangerous, to a fear-based world (I John 4:18).

So how does Jesus portray such a kingdom? He shows up riding a beast that looks as unimpressive as possible, but whose quiet strength has been tested and proven on the roughest terrains of this world. Donkeys are typically seen as laughable creatures. Compared to majestic horses, they seem, well, insignificant. Hence the incongruity of a world Savior arriving in town on one. G.K. Chesterton plays with this theme, turning it upside down:

> When fishes flew and forests walked,
> And figs grew upon thorn,
> Some moment when the moon was blood
> Then surely I was born.
> With monstrous head and sickening cry
> And ears like errant wings,
> The devil's walking parody
> On all four-footed things.
> The tattered outlaw of the earth,
> Of ancient crooked will;
> Starve, scourge, deride me: I am dumb,
> I keep my secret still.
> Fools, for I also had in my hour;
> One far fierce hour and sweet:
> *There was a shout about my ears,*
> *And palms before my feet* (italics added).
>
> From *The Wild Knight*, from Robert Knille, ed.,
> *As I Was Saying: A Chesterton Reader*
> (Grand Rapids, Mich., Eerdmans, 1985)

The humble, as it were, have the last laugh. They will inherit the earth (Matthew 5:5). For Jesus, however, there is now only grief. As he earlier made his way to Jerusalem, seeing it then at a distance, his last words to it prophesy the doom which is to come. This is not vindication, but tearful grief filled with love: "If only you know on this of all days the things that lead to peace. But now they are hidden from your eyes" (Luke 19:42).

Jerusalem does not want a messiah of love, it wants a messiah of power. It wants a messiah that leaps from pinnacles of temples, rends the clouds of heaven, summons a vast army of angels and archangels, expels the Romans from power. Jesus offers none of that. He offers the gift of humility, so we humble ourselves before him and give him everything. He offers the gift of laughter, so we follow the Messiah who rides a donkey and invites us to "enter into the joy of the Lord"—today, and forever! And he offers us peace, by making our peace with him and with all we haven't yet forgiven.

What do *you* want from him?

Prayer
Dear humble Christ of the human road, you startle us with your meekness. You overwhelm us with your tears. You empower us with your love. Over these next few days, as we walk with you toward the cross, open our hearts to this way, this truth, and this life being lived before our very eyes. Give us the grace to be more like you. We ask this in your name. Amen.

MONDAY OF HOLY WEEK
Clearing Temples

Scripture for Reflection: Matthew 21:10-17

This last Monday of Jesus' earthly life begins in the Jewish place of worship. The week began with a peaceful parade into Jerusalem, Jesus riding on the humblest beast of burden, signaling a non-violent kingdom.

Today we see another side of Jesus, a stormy side, a coercive impulse. This is no "gentle Jesus, meek and mild." This is Jesus brimming with anger.

What is the source of his explosive outburst? Has someone questioned his character, insulted him, tried to make him a laughingstock? Have his feelings been hurt, his ego undermined? Hardly. He's been living with the demeaning attacks for three tumultuous years. Jesus is provoked by something quite different: worship.

The Jesus we meet in the Gospels is a worshiper. Wherever he was on the Sabbath, he worshiped in the synagogue, or when in Jerusalem, the temple. Sometimes he was asked to read from the Hebrew Bible and make comments. Once he criticized certain Pharisees and Jewish theologians for their empty worship and shallow teaching (Mt. 15:9). You see, he was concerned about the worship of something or someone that was not God. During his wilderness temptation, he himself had to overcome the temptation to worship Satan for the material and political gain it would bring him (Luke 4:1-13).

In that day, worship was strongly identified with particular places considered sacred. In John's account of Jesus' encounter with the Samaritan woman, the woman raised the question of whether Mount Gerizim or Jerusalem was the proper center of worship. Jesus changed her question of where we worship to the question of how we worship. True worshipers will worship God, he said, "in spirit and truth" (John 4:24b). He foresaw that in his new Kingdom, any place could become holy, not by ecclesiastical designation, but by what happened there when God's people humbled themselves before Him. Jesus probably sensed that the temple in Jerusalem would not last. Rome would have had enough of Jewish resistance on the border of their empire and would destroy both city and temple later that century.

Why, then, does Jesus cause a ruckus in the temple on this Monday of the last week of his life? The prophets whom he quotes while he attacks give us a good idea. First, there is Isaiah's vision of the temple as "a house of prayer for all people," including despised immigrants and eunuchs (Isaiah 56:3-8)! Then there is Jeremiah's denunciation of those who use the temple as a cover for robbers (Jeremiah 7:11). Jesus quotes from both passages for good reason. The Court of the Gentiles is being used to exploit both poor Jewish and Gentile worshipers. Sacrificial animals are being sold to them at excessive mark-ups, and the sounds of barter are so deafening as to make worship impossible. Worship has been turned on its idolatrous head. Indeed, there is worship, but the objects are the gods of the powerful few, the gods who invite us to serve ourselves by exploiting others.

Jesus' actions seem impulsive. They are not. Mark tells us that Jesus did pay a brief visit to the temple later on the day before, the day of his triumphal entry, and then left "after he had looked around at everything" (Mark 11:11). He saw enough to disturb him, enough to rouse his righteous indignation, enough to set him at prayer that night at Bethany to bring him to a decision to clear the temple in the morning. The next day, he sets out for the temple, whip of cords in hand, with the words of Psalm 69:9 ringing in his ears: "…passion for your house has consumed me, the insults of those who insult you have fallen on me!"

The first thing he does when he enters the temple is to clear the premises of the self-servers and exploiters. For good measure he pushes over the bartering tables. Matthew records that the next thing that happens is that those who need healing now feel free to emerge from the shadows, and Jesus releases them from their oppression. Children then start finding their way closer to him, drawn to him as they always are. They shout out the words they heard the day before, "Hosanna to the Son of David!"

This was the last straw for the chief priests and theologians, those who allowed and were presiding over the desecration of worship. Jesus, they say, "Do you hear what these children are saying?" Of course, he does. And he answers them, "From the lips of children and infants/ you have ordained praise" (Psalm 8:2a, NIV). In place of the ugly sounds of aggressive commerce, the music of children announces the presence of the world-saving Messiah.

Very early in his ministry, according to John's Gospel, Jesus was consumed by a similar zeal for God's house and had acted similarly and cleared the temple. From the beginning to the end of his earthly ministry, Jesus attacks the denigration of worship. Unfortunately, worship can be confiscated by other forces, repurposed for other ends.

How and why does that happen today? It happens when we go to worship to use our church connections for our own advantage.

It happens when we want to feel okay about our comfortable lives, so we seek a congregation that looks and acts like us and worships a god that affirms the way we are living, while saving us the discomfort of the words of judgment we really need.

It happens when we go to worship to escape our problems and gain enough "good feelings" to last us the coming week, without our having to deal with the actual issues in our lives and in the world around us.

It happens when we embrace a God who only "loves us just the way we are" and desires no more of us than He is getting.

It happens, in short, when our worship masks who and what we really are in our corrupted hearts and in our self-serving living.

Imagine yourself at church on a day when Jesus bursts into the chapel and drives out those we've just described: the all-too-comfortable and complacent, the exploiters of holy places and people, the seekers of an escape from the world God loves, the habitual sinners who confess their sins with no intention of changing, and the pious pretenders. Will you and I find ourselves still there in church after Jesus' clearing is over? And if not, what will we do?

Prayer
Loving heavenly Father, I ask your forgiveness for the times I have come to worship without worshiping, bringing with me only my wants and cravings. Dear Lord Jesus, discipline me with shame for my pretense, my idolatrous worship, and help me, as your disciple, to keep your example ever before me. Blessed Holy Spirit, empower me to worship in spirit and in truth, and then to live my whole week as a recognizable extension of my worship. Amen.

TUESDAY OF HOLY WEEK
Washing Feet

Scripture for Reflection: John 13:1-19

There is more that happened this final week of Jesus' earthly life than we can include in this week of meditations. Some of them have found a place elsewhere in this book. We are going to move now to events that occurred later in Holy Week.

One of those events is that last supper Jesus shared with his disciples. Different people often remember different things about the same event, and this last supper is no exception. In particular, the remembrance of Matthew, Mark, and Luke begins with the meal itself. Jesus has sent out some of his disciples to engage a room for the Passover meal. They find a guest room on an upper level, and Jesus and his disciples gather there for their final meal together. The action begins when it's time for the meal to begin.

John's remembrance begins with a foot-washing, before the meal begins. We can take for granted that the disciples would have washed their hands before the meal, according to Jewish custom. It was also customary for the servants of the host to wash the feet of dinner guests. Walking the dusty roads in sandals made foot-washings desirable if you had just traveled a distance. Although Jesus was not the owner of the guest room, he was the host of the dinner. Without a word, he, the Master, knelt before the disciples and started washing their feet.

The disciples are struck dumb by this unexpected initiative on their Master's part. He could have asked any one of them to fulfill the task. Not until Jesus gets to Peter are words spoken: "Lord, are you going to wash *my* feet?" (italics added). Peter says what the others are thinking: Masters are not supposed to do the task of servants. (Had they forgotten Jesus' words just the week before? "The Son of Man didn't come to be served but rather to serve and to give his life to liberate many people" Matthew 20:28.) Like a parent lovingly requiring something important for the good of her child, something the value of which the child cannot yet comprehend, Jesus says he understands why Peter doesn't yet grasp the beauty and the bearing of this act, but he will later. (Perhaps a reference to Pentecost?)

Peter is not persuaded. In fact, his discomfort turns into defiance: "No! You will never wash my feet!" Jesus is quick to respond: "Unless I wash you, you won't have a place with me." Peter again misunderstands what Jesus means: "Lord, not only my feet but also my hands and my head!"

Oh Peter, don't you understand? I've already cleansed you and the others. Have these three years together meant nothing? Do you not yet understand that I am here to be not only your Master but also your Servant, not only your Mentor but also your Sacrifice. This very night the Sacrifice begins, and before six o'clock tomorrow evening, the beginning of Sabbath, the cleansing act will be complete. The spiritual bathing is happening already. It has been happening since you became my disciple and it is about to reach completion. That is why I tell you that you have bathed and are already clean. You have been with me and I have been with you, and my Spirit has been in you.

You must now prepare to walk the dusty roads of this world to declare and offer the cleansing. You will get your feet dusty with the world. You will need brothers and sisters to wash them, and you will need to wash their feet as I am washing your feet. You must never think you are above it—neither the receiving nor the giving. Never. "If I, your Lord and teacher, have washed your feet, you too must wash each other's feet...I have given you an example: just as I have done, you also must do" (John 13:14-15). The sacrifice I am about to make for you and the whole world will be a cleansing that will penetrate your heart so deeply and transform your soul so thoroughly that asking a brother or sister to wash your feet, or offering to wash their feet, will seem so... well, normal.

We who call ourselves followers and disciples of this same Jesus must remember this: Jesus washed the feet of all twelve disciples. He knew all of them would abandon him that very night. He washed the feet of every one of them! The most ardent among them would deny him to preserve his own life. Yes, he washed Peter's feet! The one named Judas was already in the process of betraying him. Yes, Jesus washed his feet! Is this our example?

What was Jesus thinking? Oh, there was no "thinking" here. Only loving in a strange new way. Genuinely being servants to those in our company we'd rather not serve, and frankly might despise. Kneel before them?

So much for us Christians who only keep company with nice Christians like us. Yes, I'll wash the feet of those I have strong affinity with, or those who think as I do, or those who appreciate me, or those I get along with, or those who are friendly. That makes the bowing down and serving not so humbling...and I certainly don't want to be humiliated by someone who would not in the least appreciate what I'm doing, kneeling before them, caring for them—and they turn it into a cruel joke.

The problem is that Jesus doesn't allow his true followers to be so choosy. He doesn't seem to see his church as a cozy society of the like-minded who attract "their kind of people," whose feet they are happy to wash. Think of Jesus' twelve: They were a classic case of an incompatible group, ranging from fishermen, to a tax collector, to a money manager, to a violent revolutionary, to who knows what else! And they didn't get along a good bit of the time! In fact, they got into an argument during this very supper about which one of them was the greatest (Luke 22:24)!

So what is Jesus asking of us, his church, today? Today, in the western world, an actual foot-washing would be a symbolic act, a teaching parable, a reminder of our calling to humble servanthood. The penetrating question for us is, "How are we going to carry out Jesus' unmistakable command: 'You too must wash each other's feet. I have given you an example: just as I have done, you also must do'" (13:14b)?

If there is anything Christians can do to transform their congregations, it is to humble themselves before God and each other—no one excluded! The foot-washing will rarely be literal. It will be delivered through our day-to-day words and actions. It will not be a one-time or even occasional event. It will be part of our daily living. It will be our calling we never outgrow! For the rest of our lives, and for eternity.

Prayer
Dear Jesus, I thank you for the gift of your example, and for the empowerment through your Spirit I so much need. Humble Savior, make me, one way or the other, a washer of feet. Lower me before the congregation where I worship and serve, and especially before those who make the humbling most difficult for me. Rob me of my pride and bless me with your humility in the presence of others. I pray this in your name, the name of the lowly Nazarene my Savior, Jesus the Christ. Amen.

WEDNESDAY OF HOLY WEEK
Breaking His Heart

Scripture for Reflection: Mark 14:32-42

Jesus and his disciples have shared their final supper together, a Passover meal laden with the flavor of God's deliverance for His people. Yesterday, we shared John's remembrance of foot-washing just before the meal. The other three Gospel writers focus on the meal itself. Midway through that meal, Jesus makes a disturbing revelation. With profound sadness he says, "I assure you that one of you will betray me." And then, as if to make it very concrete: "someone eating with me" right now.

How are his disciples supposed to react to that bombshell? "Deeply saddened, they ask him one by one, 'It's not I, is it?'" Hmm, why did every one of them have to ask? My guess is that, deep down, they all knew they were capable of it. After all, later that evening they would all abandon him to his enemies.

Who is it, Jesus? And all Jesus says is: "It's one of the twelve who is dipping bread with me into his bowl." But Jesus, that's all of us! Why can't you say who?

Oh, how we love to be able to identify the worst among us, so that we can heap our contempt on him, belittle him, feel so much above him, appear better than him. Build ourselves up because we know without admitting it, that we have our own flaws. "Jesus, point him out, so we can feel better about ourselves." And Jesus won't. He refuses to betray the very one he knows is already betraying him, the very one who is breaking his heart. And surprisingly, he grieves the terrible price that betrayer will pay at the end.

What follows is the covenant act: Jesus, breaking and sharing the bread, taking the cup, and offering it to his disciples. "Take; this is my body; and this is my blood of the covenant, which is poured out for many." And when they have partaken, they sing their last song together—probably a Passover hymn, a hymn they will later come to realize is now about a different Lamb, one who was to be slain for the world's deliverance. Their Lord Jesus, the Lamb of God.

And then they go through the city gates and cross the Kidron Valley to the Mount of Olives, while Judas sneaks off to help Jesus' enemies find him. Here, in the shadow of those olive trees that seem to endure forever as testimony, Jesus tells his remaining eleven that they will all falter in their faithfulness to him. Ah, they are not so perfect after all! We're not surprised that Peter won't admit it: "Even if I must die alongside you, Jesus, I will not deny you." Not to be outdone, the others join in: "Uh yea, we're all with you, Jesus." And it breaks Jesus' heart.

The company then moves to the other side of the Mount of Olives, to the place called Gethsemane, a garden forever memorialized as the place where Jesus' heartbreak reached its peak. From there on, the questioning and the pleas end: After Gethsemane, Jesus is set for humiliation, untold public and physical abuse, and crucifixion.

Let's not, however, take Gethsemane for granted, as if it were simply "the next phase" on the way to the cross. If anyone is prone to question Jesus' humanity, as if his human flesh was simply a garb for divinity, he or she needs to hear the heart cries of Jesus in this garden. Taking Peter, James, and John with him, he asks them to stay a distance and keep watch while he prays. He has begun to feel a deep despair, a profound anxiety. "I'm very sad," he says to them. "It's as if I'm dying." He goes a little further and falls to the ground.

He lifts his helpless hands to heaven, like a small child to his father, and pleads, "Abba—Daddy—Father, for you all things are possible. Take this cup of suffering away from me." Please, is it really too late? Isn't there some other way? Some other direction? Some other solution? That's what I would like, I have to admit it. But in the end, Abba, it's not what I want, but what you want.

I doubt that God "wanted" it, as if He took any pleasure whatsoever in Jesus' suffering and brutal death. No, I believe Abba God experienced the pain as poignantly and profoundly as did His Son—and if you don't believe that, I think you've got the Trinity all wrong.

Jesus returns to his three friends to find them fast asleep and not keeping watch, much less praying. Three times in all, he returns to find them sleeping. He reminds them to "stay alert and pray so that you won't give in to temptation. The spirit is eager, but the flesh is weak." The final time he says to them: "Will you sleep and rest all night? That's enough! The time has come for the Human One [the Son of Man] to be betrayed into the hands of sinners. Get up! Let's go! Look, here comes my betrayer."

Surprisingly, this evening Jesus is not hard on his disciples. He does warn them of the danger of their inattentiveness. But we know his heart is broken. They have failed him many times, and he knows they will fail him again.

Meanwhile, Judas has calculated correctly. He knows Jesus and the others will be there in the garden. Even before Jesus has finished speaking, a gathering storm can be heard, and soon it bursts upon them, surrounding them, taunting them. Who are they? Judas and a band of temple guards and ruffians carrying swords and clubs, sent by, yes, the religious authorities. Judas lifts his hand to silence the mob. He gives the guards these simple instructions: "Arrest the man I kiss and take him away under guard."

Judas doesn't sound like someone in charge. His voice cracks, because his heart is broken, too. Broken by his own inability to grasp a messiah that loves beyond the borders. A messiah that has compassion for each individual rather than one with a political agenda to make things right. A messiah who changes hearts and lives, rather than redistributes power. Judas just can't bring himself to believe in that kind of a messiah. He's given Jesus plenty of time to prove he can get the messianic job done the right way. But after three years of kingdom talk and attention focused on the little people, where is this new movement today? "Nowhere. Jesus, I've grown to love you, but I can't trust you to do what messiahs are supposed to do. So I have to bring it all to an end. And it breaks my heart because I know you love me so much, and you will still love me—in spite of what I have done."

Can you betray someone you love? You can. And Judas does it with a kiss. Jesus' heart has been breaking; now it is broken. Broken for us all. You and me. Even those of us who strive so hard to be like him, so that our living and our loving will suggest him to others. And sometimes we don't do it well at all. Sometimes we really muck it up. Sometimes, yes sometimes, we break his heart. And always, yes always, he forgives.

He forgives! That is the power that is released that day, from the crucified One whose heart we have broken. That is the good news to betrayers, cowards, unfaithfuls, deserters, and backsliders: Jesus' heart was broken, and his life was given for the likes of us.

Prayer

Abba, Father, thank you for giving us Jesus. Dear Jesus, thank you for taking us in as we are, with all the disappointments we bring, knowing up front we would sometimes fail you, maybe even betray you. Thank you for a deep forgiveness that leaves us stronger rather than weaker. Thank you for your Holy Spirit that sanctifies our hearts and guides our living. And finally, Lord, may our own hearts become broken for this world you love. We pray in your Name. Amen.

THURSDAY OF HOLY WEEK
Being Thirsty

Scripture for Reflection: John 19:16-30

"I'm thirsty." In John's Gospel these oh-so-human words were the next-to-the-last words of Jesus. *I...am...thirsty.*

Why did John put this in his Gospel? John, this elegant theologian who could speak of the Word of God becoming flesh and making his home with us, and of seeing glory like that of a father's only son, full of grace and truth (John 1:14). So eloquent and glorious, it sends chills up the spine of a believer. And then we come to the end of this story of our incarnate God, and the next-to-his-last words, says John, are "I'm thirsty"—like some child coming in from play on a hot day: "Mama, I'm so thirsty." Why does John include this desperate cry of a very human Jesus?

Do you think maybe he put it there for *us*? Jesus didn't have a problem with being human, but maybe *we* do. Get outta here! I'm fully aware "I'm only human." I'm fully aware I've got limitations to overcome. I wish I *weren't* so...human.

And Jesus says to us, "I wish you were *more* human. The Father *made* you human, and I'm here," says Jesus, "to show you *how* to be human, how to be what the Father made you to be." Get rid of that stupid notion that your human limitations are the *cause* of your sin. The cause of your sin is that you want to *exceed* those limitations. How did the snake in the Garden put it: "Bite the forbidden apple of my temptation, and you shall become *as God*! Unencumbered by your human limitations!"

Brothers and sisters, we have a saving gospel because, as the apostle Paul put it, God "emptied Himself" down to our human limitations:

- Jesus became poor—so why do we go after more and more and more material possessions and pretensions?

- Jesus hung out with the common people, the outcasts, the sick, the marginalized—so, why are we so impressed with the high-flyers, the wealthy, the people in "positions"…and why do we feel so important ourselves when we are around them, maybe even pretending to *be* them?

- Jesus suffered—so why do we complain about *our* suffering, some people on a daily basis?

- Jesus failed with so many people—so why do we let *our* failures defeat and embitter us?

- Jesus was tempted as we are—so why are we surprised or alarmed or disarmed over *our* temptations?

- Jesus loved to share a meal with his disciples—so why do we eat and run to get "important things" done, when in truth we are so impoverished that we really do need to connect with the person sitting across from us.

Jesus became poor so we could all own up to our own impoverishment. We are the neediest creatures of God's creation. Eugene Peterson says it this way: "When God became human in Jesus, he showed us how to become complete human beings before him. We do it the way Jesus did, by becoming absolutely needy and dependent on the Father. Only when we stand emptied, stand impoverished before God can we receive what only empty hands can receive…[In truth] we are all beggars" (Tell It Slant, 54-55).

Brothers and sisters, we're all impoverished, or we're not

human. We all have limits and need help. Some of our limits are the same—we all thirst, we hunger, we hurt, we wish "if only I had done this or that, or not done this or that…" We all have a limited life span on this earth, only so much time to love each other, to ask for forgiveness, to help each other, perhaps to give our perfectionist self a break or two, or perhaps finally to get serious about life. We only have so much time to get to know God so we can love Him even more, or perhaps resolve a problem we have with Him.

And each of us has impoverishments that are unique to us. Every one of us. A number of years ago, Keitha and I had the privilege of going to an elementary school play called "Don't Rock the Boat." We wanted to go because our grandson, Ryan, was one of the main characters. He's very shy, but he had an inspiration and decided he really wanted to be in the play. When he was told he would play the part of the captain of the ship, he got cold feet. Heather, his mother, held those cold feet to the fire, and I say—as an impartial judge, of course—he played his part very well.

There's something else about that play I want to tell you about. I want to tell you about the girl who played the part of Honey Hotchkiss, the fabulous, beautiful, snobbish Hollywood actress, one of the passengers on the fictional cruise ship. Let's call her Grace (not her real name). Grace was one of those children with some obvious physical limitations. Both her hands were bent inward, with shortened fingers; her legs were partially disabled, causing her to walk only in a kind of sideways manner. And some of her facial muscles were underdeveloped.

Why in the world did the director choose her to play the part of Honey Hotchkiss? Surely, it will embarrass her, and make the audience embarrassed for her.

Embarrass her? Embarrass the audience? That director turned out to be a genius. When Honey Hotchkiss made her first entrance, she sashayed across that stage with her flaming red hair making her look as if she were on fire—and she was. She carried herself as if she owned the place—and she did own the place, and she owned us. She convinced and she glowed in every scene she played.

Most people don't have Grace's specific physical limitations: they are unique to her. But every one of us has his or her own impoverishments. Every one of us. We may use them for an excuse, or even to garner pity, or even to help us feel more self-righteous because of our "burden."

Or we may decide to look at Jesus on the cross, impoverished of just about everything save his Father's love and the love of that small band of disciples and loved ones—and we can hear him say, "I'm thirsty." Confessing and owning this most basic human need. Made utterly helpless by his love for us.

"I'm thirsty"—this is God speaking, for heaven's sake. God becoming human, being human, dying human—so that we could live out what it means to be fully human, and fully holy—to the glory of God!

And then Jesus said, "It's done, finished, completed!" Thanks be to God!

Prayer

Dear Lord Jesus, thank you for giving us back the humanity which our sin had robbed us of. Give us the humility to accept our limitations so that we can find the true gifts behind them. As you became a human to show us holiness, we seek your Holy Spirit's gift of holiness, so that we can show those around us how to discover their true humanity in you. I pray this in your name, the name of our perfectly human Savior, Son of our ever-loving God. Amen.

GOOD FRIDAY
Gifting Paradise

Scripture for Reflection: Luke 23:32-43

For one brief moment, the agony of a tortuous six-hour death is interrupted by a word of hope—one bright beam of light against a grim background. Before that, Jesus is jeered: "If you really are the King of the Jews, save yourself!" And it will all end with the terrible darkness seeming to cover the whole earth. But in between, one dying man offers everything to another dying man.

What does a dying man think about? Certainly he thinks about himself: what he's done, or left undone, how he's going to face his death. Certainly he thinks about the loved ones he's leaving behind. Jesus had a whole world to think about, a world of people whose future depended on the death he was dying. The future of humankind hung on that cross.

What does Jesus do at this moment? He freezes time, brings everything to a stop…to say to one very unworthy criminal, right to his face, "I assure you that today you will be with me in paradise."

Let's let that interruption take effect.

Consider the word "today." Not some far-off tomorrow. Today. When Jesus speaks that word, the man enters a new kingdom. John Bunyan described his own conversion as seeing himself in heaven and earth at once.

What is heaven? Listen to Jesus' words: "…today you will be with me…" Is this what heaven is, then? Primarily. If it's not primarily that, then it isn't much of anything else. In Psalm 27: 4, David pleads: "I have asked one thing from the Lord—it's all I seek—to live in the Lord's house all the days of my life, seeing the Lord's beauty and constantly adoring his temple."

Or we can recall the verse from one of Bramwell Booth's songs:

> Thyself alone wilt make my heaven
> Though all thy gifts remove.

And the apostle Paul is not far from these sentiments when he says to the Thessalonian church: "Jesus died for us so that, whether we are awake or asleep, we will live together with him" (I Thess. 5:10). And he gets personal with the Philippian Christians when he writes to them: "I want to leave this life and be with Christ, which is far better" (Philippians 1:23b). "Where you are, [Lord]," said Thomas a Kempis, "*there* is heaven; and where you are not, behold there [is] death and hell" (*Imitation of Christ*).

"Today you will be with me *in paradise*," says Jesus to the man. Who knows where that is? We only know *what* it is. It's the place of blessedness. It's the place where grace is everywhere. It's the place where only grace can bring you. It's the home we go to—by the way of the Cross.

The Cross. This means that the man named Jesus is not only under the sentence of death, he is also under the sentence of a criminal. Early in his ministry, Jesus had been sharply criticized for associating with the worst sorts of sinners. And now here, during his last hours, during the very drama of his death, he is still solidly in their company—one sinner on his right and one on his left.

Let's not take him out of their company and try to lock him up inside stained glass walls. "The Son of Man came to seek and to save those who are lost." The picture stands indelibly painted against the background of history: *three* crosses on a hill—the Savior and two sinners at his sides. He includes himself among them, so that they can be included with him. He shares their suffering so that they can share in his resurrection joy. The promise of paradise is given by one crucified man to another.

He is a robber, a bandit, possibly an insurrectionist. Oh yes, attempts have sometimes been made to romanticize him and make him into a nice guy who got caught with the wrong crowd—which would logically explain his "natural" attraction to Jesus. The record allows no such fantasizing. He is a criminal, and Mark's Gospel tells us further that at one point earlier he throws his jeers at Jesus, too.

Now, by what right does Jesus give *him* a place in the kingdom of God? By what right is a common criminal, during the last moments of his wasted life, allowed to share in the same inheritance shared by those who have labored for the Master from the dawn to the setting sun?

By grace, through faith, that not of himself: the gift of God. "Today, you who make no claims to earning your salvation, you who come up with no proof you're worth saving: *You* will be with me in paradise."

Here on a cross, it suddenly becomes clear to a dying criminal that his life has been futile, and he deserves no more than death. This was no last-ditch effort to appear humble before God. Growing tired of his own jeering, he begins to watch Jesus. He recognizes a man who in no way deserves this fate. So why is he accepting it? Why is he taking this suffering alongside *me*? Why?

Just listen to him! He even wants his executioners to be forgiven. I heard him! How do you kill that kind of love? I'll bet the world will not hear the last of this Jesus. "Jesus, remember me when you come into your kingdom."

Remember me: a modest request. No doubt he felt he had no

right to ask even that. But if only Jesus could remember him. If only he were not cast out into the endless sea of time and space, swallowed into oblivion. A nobody.

Jesus was ready to give him remembrance, and far more: "Today you will be with me in paradise." The grace of God for a man who has nothing to bring but empty hands.

The text doesn't tell us the criminal's response. It doesn't need to. We know what happened: a nobody of that day became a somebody for eternity. "The forgotten of men became the never-to-be-forgotten of God" (Paul Scherer).

There's a verse from an old gospel song we used to sing:

> Are you able to remember, when a thief lifts up his eyes,
> That his pardoned soul is worthy of a place in paradise?
> Lord, we are able, our spirits are thine;
> Remold them, make us like thee divine.

Prayer
Dear Lord, we thank You that You numbered yourself among transgressors like us. And now, by the endless merits of your cross and through the grace of your forgiving love, we now stand redeemed, members of your family, heirs of your promise. Thank you. Help us never to take this gift for granted, nor to withhold it from those around us. In the name of Jesus, our Savior from sin and our Model for living, Amen.

HOLY SATURDAY
Tasting Death

Scripture for Reflection: John 19:38-42

Jesus is now dead, his body hanging limp, like a rag doll, from the crude wooden cross. The humiliation is now complete, the pain gone. He is a body, a thing. Others will take over and do things to that body, and he has no say in it. He will likely be thrown in some graveyard ditch reserved for criminals, a burial with no decency.

Will someone come forward to claim his body for a more decent burial? Where is his close band of disciples who have displayed such courage as his loyal followers over these last three years? All of them gone, huddled in fear behind closed doors (John 20:19). Is there not anyone who will care for the body of our Lord? After all he's gone through? No one who has loved so deeply deserves to have his body abandoned to chance.

There is a man named Joseph, from Arimathea. Never heard of him. He's a man of some means, says Matthew's Gospel (Matthew 27:57), a prominent member of the Jewish Council who eagerly anticipates the coming of God's kingdom, says Mark's Gospel (15:43). John's Gospel calls him "a disciple of Jesus, but a secret one because he feared the Jewish authorities" (John 19:38). Ah, another coward.

Wait, he's coming forward! He has the gall to approach Pilate and offer to dispose of Jesus' body! "Don't you know, Joseph, this will get you in trouble, if not with Rome's man in Jerusalem, certainly with the religious authorities? Your coveted seat on the Council will be in serious jeopardy." As it turns out, Pilate is happy to be rid of the last remnant of this troublesome Messiah.

"Yes, take him. I want to hear no more of him."

What has overcome a cowardly Joseph? Perhaps he was present for the crucifixion. Perhaps that was where things started to come together for him. Perhaps he finally began to see how the kingdom of God he was looking for would become reality. Looking into the suffering face of his Messiah, he may have seen the power of God's love and realized that this was the force that would conquer the world, beginning with the likes of a coward like him. Joseph knew of "a new tomb in which no one had been laid," in a garden near where Jesus had just been crucified, and the man from Arimathea had the money to buy it. There "they laid Jesus."

You may remember there are two Josephs in Jesus' story. The first is Joseph, husband of Mary and adoptive father of Jesus. The man who protects Mary's honor, nurtures the child Jesus, teaches him the carpenter trade—and then disappears from the Gospel record in Jesus' twelfth year, not a word from his mouth recorded in that whole record. The second is Joseph of Arimathea, from whom also no words are recorded. Out of fear of the consequences, he has not spoken a public word of his faith in Jesus—until now, when the courage of Calvary took him over. Two quiet men named Joseph, each playing an important role in the story of Jesus—one at the beginning, the other at the end of the Savior's earthly life. We know nothing more about them. God knows everything about them. He honors the quiet people, especially those least recognized for their behind-the-scenes contributions to His kingdom.

Speaking of people behind the scenes, let's not forget Nicodemus, who seems to appear out of nowhere with "a mixture of myrrh and aloe." He and Joseph take Jesus' body, anoint it with the spices, and wrap it in linen for burial. Nicodemus is surely in the process of becoming a follower of Jesus (See John 3:1-21; 7:50-52), and the risk of his action this very day seems to seal the matter. And let's not forget the brave women, seemingly untouched by the fear that paralyzed most of the men, remaining at the cross, the agonizing sounds of their weeping a public testimony: Jesus' mother Mary, Mary Magdalene, Joanna, Mary the mother of James, and other women who have accompanied Jesus' group from Galilee—some of them appearing at the tomb early Sunday morning, bringing their own offering, more spices for the body of their Lord. Stubbornly faithful women, standing with their Messiah to the end, perhaps somehow sensing this may not be the end but some kind of beginning.

How can this be? How can death be the beginning of anything? Our bodies deteriorate over most of our lives. We call it aging, and aging will sooner or later bring us to the point where our body can no longer sustain our life. We die. As one of us, Jesus died. He experienced death, real death. It was an early martyr's death to be sure, but the Gospel records make clear that on the cross he actually did die. Heretics uncomfortable with this fact began to insist that before Jesus died, the divine Christ departed from his physical body. Those who espoused this view thought that the human body was by nature evil (also a heresy!); it meant, they said, that Jesus' body was simply temporary defective garb. This meant that the divine Christ could not possibly participate in the death of Jesus. In other words, the person Jesus was not really two-natured, both fully God and fully man united. The divine could not really suffer death. The Son of God was totally removed from the dying Jesus.

Heresy, say Scripture and the church creed: "He was crucified under Pontius Pilate, dead and buried." Why is the death of Jesus important? What is there for us to say this Holy Saturday, the time between Jesus' death on Friday and his resurrection on Sunday? Is it only raw flesh that lies in the tomb? Are we today simply marking time, waiting for what we now know to be the outcome on Sunday? Or did something actually happen on this Holy Saturday?

Yes, something did happen. Jesus experienced death, as we all must: as a bondage, the ultimate wages of sin, the finale of the curse. Good Friday is when we remember the horror of Jesus dying; today is when we experience the reality of it. Jesus not only touched death, he tasted it.

There is something else about Jesus' death: Even here, Jesus never gives up his mission. Peter, quoting from Psalm 16 in his Pentecost sermon, says, "...my body will live in hope, because [the Lord] won't abandon me to the grave (Acts 2:26c-27). Later, Peter suggests that from the grave, Jesus actually preached the good news to the dead who "were judged as humans according to human standards" so that "they could live by the Spirit according to divine standards" (I Peter 4:6). The earliest Christian creed picked this up with the phrase that became part of the church's confession of faith, "He descended into hell." In the hours of his own death, Jesus keeps to his saving mission.

Jesus stays with us to and through the end. He will stay with us where and when our bodies are placed in the grave. And this is why we stay with him on this Saturday, just as he stayed with those who, though dead, still needed him. This is one of the Bible's mysteries. We don't need to grasp it with our minds, but with our hearts we see Jesus as he is, loving and saving—wherever and whenever he is.

Prayer

Ever living Lord Jesus, today we honor those who cared for you in your death, while others stayed away out of fear. Whatever my own fears about death or dying, please grant me the assurance that you will be present with me when the time comes. Help me never to take the days of my life for granted, nor to forget the possibility that death could come on any day and in whatever way. When I do face my own death, in spite of the uncertainties that may plague me, open my eyes to see you waiting to accompany me, and give me the grace to release those I so love and free them even more to become who they are in Christ. I pray this in your name, who faced death for me. Amen.

EASTER SUNDAY
Resurrection Awakening

Scripture for Reflection: Matthew 28:1-10, 16-20

Jesus has died, and Mary Magdalene and the other Mary have come to pay their last respects and anoint the body with precious spices. They are grieving. There had been so much promise for a new tomorrow, and now only memories. Only shattered dreams. Only lost hope.

Maybe people were right about Jesus' kingdom of God—the religious realists who dismissed it, the doubters who ridiculed it, the power structures who killed it, the ones who criminalized, condemned, and crucified the hope. They shattered the dream. Even Jesus' closest followers seemed to be calling it quits. Still, the women came.

"Let's just anoint his body one last time." The Marys want to say a final farewell to their Lord, perhaps to keep the memories of what could have been and now seems lost. To honor the dream.

But perhaps there is still a thread of lingering confidence. Perhaps the women see past the overwhelming evidence of failure to a glimmer of awakening hope, and they cling to it and nurture it deep down, in their quiet way. A part of them remains open to a different outcome, to a Jesus who will not let them down.

The tomb greets them in a most unsettling way: a violent earthquake accompanied by a powerful angel, who rolls away the huge stone blocking and sealing the tomb, and then seats himself on it and looks at the two ladies with a calming face. (The guards are cowering in fear.) "Don't be afraid," says the angel. "He isn't here because he's been raised from the dead, just as he said."

What is this? What does this strange person mean? "Come, see the place where they laid him," he says. The women follow him. They are aghast at what they see. Who has stolen the body—and where is it now? Wait, this angel just said the crucified Jesus has been raised from the dead. But where did he go? That, by the way, is the question they will from then on pursue and answer for the rest of their lives, as will we. But for the time being, "You'll see him in Galilee," says the angel. "Right now, your job is to go find his disciples, who are probably pitying themselves, and tell them the good news."

Suddenly realizing the importance of this shocking revelation, "with great fear and excitement," the women hurry off to tell the disciples. There's another surprise for them soon after they depart. A bigger surprise. Jesus is waiting for them along the way. Stunned by the sight of him, they fall, grab his feet, and worship him.

What is it like to be the first humans to worship the resurrected Jesus? What shall they do, and how shall they do it? Without the obstruction of theological rationale or debate, they simply follow their deepest instinct and largest love—they bow, they cling, they adore.

And thus begins this lifetime journey for all the awakened Easter people. The Easter people: those who wake up every day to the reality of a resurrected Jesus, wherever they may be on their journey. Those whose lives will now be changed over a lifetime by the Jesus they remember and study, who now lives. Those awakened with eyes to see their resurrected Lord and ears to hear his voice and hearts to resonate more and more with his.

Holy Week closes with a deceased Jesus. This first Easter day, the Christians' new Sabbath, opens with a living Jesus—not a resuscitation, a resurrection! Jesus with an eternal body. The bonds of the grave are torn asunder and the burst of a new life emerges. Having lived our earthly life with us for over thirty years and having tasted death for us, he brings to life a new thing, a first, a resurrection. He awakens not as he fell asleep in death; he awakens clothed with eternity.

We have been on a Lenten journey over the past forty-six days. We have studied Jesus. We have allowed him to reveal who we are and who we need to become. We have been humbled by his humility. Our need for his healing and for his re-creating work in our lives has been exposed. We have seen how important to our holy humanity are our brothers and sisters in Christ, as well as those who are not in our fellowship. We have walked Jesus' last week with him, culminating with his life poured out for us on a cross and in his death. Where do we go from here?

We'll follow the story. We'll follow those disciples who obey and go to Galilee, to the place Jesus tells them to go. Like some of them, we may have doubts (28:17). But we still go looking to find him where he said he would be. He comes close to us because we take the risk of obedience and follow him. The obedience may be slow in coming, owing to our own unreadiness at first, or our uncertainty, or our doubt. But then, sooner or later, a peace comes, and then an awakening. We're now ready to meet our calling from Jesus:

> I've received all authority in heaven and on earth. Therefore, go and make disciples of all nations [ethnicities], baptizing them in the name of the Father, and of the Son, and of the Holy Spirit, teaching them to obey everything that I've commanded you. Look, I myself will be with you every day until the end of this present age (28:18b-20).

This is the calling of every disciple of Jesus, every person who claims to be a Christian. Every follower of Jesus, in one way or another, follows him into the world, whether that world is as close as the neighbors on our street or as far away as the other side of the globe. We are all sent into the world to act like and speak for the living Christ.

During this Lenten season, we have been awakened by Jesus to see ourselves and one another. We have looked at the good in us as well as the bad. We have prayed for ourselves, for one another, for those we like and those we don't like, and for the world. What is the power of those prayers? We pray them in the name of our crucified, resurrected, and living Lord Jesus. The Cross releases the saving power of love, the resurrection brings the miracle of life eternal, and the Spirit gifts us with accessibility to the living Jesus and through him to the Father. This power, this miracle, and this intimacy with God are together the keys we've been given to live the life of Jesus in the world.

We are Christ's awakeners, called to lead the awakening wherever we live our lives. We heed the call: "Wake up, sleeper! Get up from the dead, and Christ will shine on you" (Ephesians 5:14b). We are bearers of the light-revealing Light of the world. We are driven by that same question on the minds of the two women: "Where has Jesus gone?" We, like they, really want to find the living Lord. We set out in faith, and on the way of our obedience he appears, and as we love him and worship him, the way before us begins to become clear. So does our calling as his awakeners. Our lives, our words, become a wake-up call and an invitation to those we meet along the way. This is the fulfillment of our lives.

Prayer

Living, loving Lord, I give myself to the joy of finding you in the unexpected places of my life, representing you where you are treated as unknown or misunderstood, speaking of you where current words are unhelpful or demeaning, and being you where sin and hopelessness diminish our humanity. May my life help to awaken those I meet to your presence and your love. I pray this in your name and for your sake. Amen.

Works Cited

Buechner, Frederick, *Listening to Your Life*. Compiled by George Conner. HarperSanFrancisco, 1992.

Celtic Daily Prayer: Book Two—Farther Up and Farther In. London: Harper Collins, 2015.

Chesterton, G. K., *The Wild Knight*, from Robert Knille, ed., *As I Was Saying: A Chesterton Reader*. Grand Rapids, Michigan: Eerdmans, 1985.

Frost, Robert, "Mending Wall," *The Poetry of Robert Frost*. Henry Holt and Company, 1969.

Ignatius, *Epistles of Ignatius*, v. 50-52.

Needham, Phil, *Following Rabbi Jesus: The Christian's Forgotten Calling*. Eugene, Oregon: Wipf and Stock, 2018

Peterson, Eugene, *Tell It Slant*. Grand Rapids: Eerdmans, 2008.

Poxon, Peter J., ed., *Through the Year with Catherine Booth*. Oxford, UK: Monarch Books, 2016.